AARON'S POEMS

TWO YEARS IN THE MAKING

DISCLAIMER
Most of the poems or songs are based on real life experiences like there being a corona virus pandemic or being hardbroken also some are completely fictional.

Any people's names mentioned like melody are fictional I don't know a melody or anyone else I have written about their names were purely plucked out at random so I had someone to talk about in the poem or song. If you are reading this and I have mentioned your name don't worry it was written about you purely coincidentally.

CONTENTS
I am not doing a content because each poem is about a different topic/subject. Therefore, it would take hours and hours. Look at it like this each page will be a surprise so if you don't like one poem or song, then don't worry as you might like the next or vice versa.

DEDICATION
Thank you to my mum for looking after me throughout this hard time everyone is going through the pandemic and of course thanks to my carers and sitter who have looked after me while I have been recovering from my operation on my ankle that I had in September 2020.

First published in United Kingdom 2021.

If I get a lot of reviews of this book that are good and are from legitimate news and entertainment sources I shall post a second edition of this book will extra content and more poems and songs.

OTHER BOOKS FROM THIS AUTHOR:
HALLOWEEN: AN AUTUMN RIVERS MYSTERY

10 9 8 7 6 5 4 3 2 1

The Outsider

You start out at square one,
Everyone starts at zero they say,
Just like a Rubik's cube there are many
Different combinations that you can take,
Once you have chosen the way you want like to go,
There is a band who put on a show,
For the audience so why do you feel alone,
In a fully packed theatre you feel cold,
You feel like the mould on the edges of the block of cheese that went off
months ago.

It's just like being on the outline of the friend's circle,
Yes, Ribena is purple,
Existing as an outsider on that cold fall evening,
Barely surviving as a human being,

You have had your name on display,
All day, look a little closer for the closer meaning,
One closer to being someone who means
to be something to someone.

What the SIMPSONS did not predict,
Is that my happiness was down to sequences of numbers that out of context
meant nothing,
You are bluffing to saving your life,
Let alone you searching for a wife.

You hover around the helipad,
Wanting one of the people getting off
To say next time, you can fly with us!
Instead of getting that old ratchet bus.

This person I could call a friend,
Just like a hen with their coup.

Amazing

I just read my podcast review on iTunes,
I am over the moon the first five star I got,
Was in August last year,
If I was to cry they would be happy tears,
I never told anyone what to say,
That has made my month so far,
Like the Jonas Blue cover of fast car.

When I did not have my disability,
We were all on holiday and this bloke kept singing fast car,
Dad was saying that is your friend,
Haha, no he is not I said but I have never seen Tracy Chapman,
Have you?
I was feeling blue.

I miss my dad,
He did not talk much,
Especially not over lunch,
However, he watched what I watched,
Which was the chase,
We used to compete against each other,
Sometimes he would finish the ladder first,
Now when I complete the ladder on the show,
I am thinking oh do not go for the low offer,

Dad used to find it an insult to his intelligence,
So, I took the high offer of 28K completed the ladder,
Then beat the beast in the final chase,
If only it was real money,
That would nearly be just as honey,
I aint even being funny!

Thirty

I heard that your 20s are all about trying to figure out your teenage years,
Looking back were your 20s better than your teens,
If so why? I don't know,
Oh, LOOK those pins and I aint talking skittles,
Your legs are so inviting I want to taste them,
So, I pull your shirt down from its hem,

What I was saying your thirties are definitely flirty,
Do you like it clean or dirty?
You just hit thirty worry about work later,
I want you now on a theoretical platter,
Your body is my breakfast, lunch and dinner,
No matter whether you are thin, fat or with that extra skin to cuddle up too,

More to cuddle in the winter months,
Oh, oops here come the hiccups,
I'll let you take control of me anytime,
Every time is prime time for me when I think of you,
Who? It could be anyone but it's not it's for you,
It's true.
Just like cows say moo, moo, moo,
Ghosts are known to say boo, boo, boo,

Thirty is the new forty,
So, what are you going to do,
Will you reinvent yourself,
I aint talking lip fillers or Botox to get rid of your bags,
Under your eyes,
Just cut down on the fries,
Your ticker is counting down as you read this,
So, forget the haters it's time to get down to business,

By business, I mean having cocktails but not too many,
Don't worry I don't even feel I have had a drink,
I know my limits and I stuck to them,

You know what I mean,
I'm very keen,
Well f**k then use the Mr. Sheen,
Meditate afterwards to practice being a doctor,
As your spleen controls your bile,
If you are sick too-often,
Your spleen keeps your bile clean,
If you wear it out,
Like anything it will malfunction,

I aint talking s***,
Google it.

Sweet as Sugar

Sometimes it's not only sweet food like doughnuts that you indulge in,
Sweetness can be a form of happiness like dopamine,
Obviously, you want it to continue so what do you do?
Well I'll give a clue,
Watch your favourite TV show,
Or one of you favourite films,
Or going to your local gym,
If you're a man you are probably thinking I want to look like him,
That's my goal,

I want to be able to say,
'Welcome to the gun show',
No, I don't mean guns I mean these puppies,
As he points to his biceps,
You know what they say,
No pain, no gain,

I am clever but not that attractive,
I don't intent to be,
I just want to be me,
It's that saying,
Since the big bang theory,
Being an intelligent person,
Makes you a hit with the ladies,
There are no maybes,

Even people who didn't how to speak to ladies,
Ended up getting laid with some southern birds,
A little birdie told me,
Whatever floats your boat,
I can turn you your favourite quote into a tote,
I'd love for you to motorboat,
My baps, they are bloomers,

Almost anything can sound dirty without even trying,
I really hope I can go abroad,
Although that nurse made upset,
She said if you had AstraZeneca it would cause blood clots,
As the plane flies about thirty-thousand feet,
I only want to see my friends from Clapper,
Even at the meet in the UK, I can't because I need a community carer,

To wheel me anywhere I tell them too.

Truth or Dare

It's the month when all of the monsters, ghouls and ghosts,
Come out of the graveyard and stalk their family that are still alive,
Don't choose dare; always choose truth because they could dare you,
To invite spirits into the house.

What I mean by that is don't say Bloody Mary three times in the mirror,
You will conjure her spirit up from the graveyard,
Why are horror films shorter than any other genre?
People can't bare getting scared for longer,
Also, some people linger and not focus on the film.

Some people walk out of the film half way through,
For a good reason they were s*** scared,
They thought it was lucky they were out of there,
They went back home cuddled their teddy bears.

I have to admit me and mum walked out of Drag Me to Hell,
I was like f**k that for a laugh,
Wait why is there is a draft,
All of a sudden, it's got cold,
I don't think I'm bold,
Enough is enough,

That was before my disability,
The characters in the TV show Supernatural,
They were talking about that movie,
Like it was nothing scary at all,
What have they got stones for hearts?
This is what people are like in the year 2021,
A little scare never scared anyone to death,
As far as I know, oh hold on let's back track,

Heath Ledger couldn't separate himself from the Joker
He played,
I don't scare easily but his version was so bloody scary,
I can believe it.
That's right I said I can believe it because
When he was playing the Joker,
He had to get into character which he probably hated,
If you ask me to play him and wear that make up,
I would be like f**k off,

No way,
Not for all of the money in the world.

Lovely or Lonely?

If you won the lottery would you really be happy?
You would be carrying the weight of the world on your shoulders,
Meaning are they just being nice to me because they want some of my money,
I mean if money was dripping from you like runny honey,
You would suddenly have an abundance of people wanting to be your friend,
So, if this was the case you would be a millionaire but who would be happy the richest man in the world living alone,
Or the binman who has a wife and children?

How do you manage wealth?
How do you manage health?
You never asked for this,
Whatcha going to do now,
Will you be that the person who dies alone,
Or will you be that person will thousands of cards saying get well soon,
Tonight, is a new moon,
Time for a new beginning,
Who will be in it though,
You have got all that dough,

Will you be a philanthropist?
Will you be very generous,
Or will you be as tight as extra skinny jeans,
If you know what I mean,
Will you work 9 to 5,
Hardly talk to your family,
When that is the whole reason you are working,
In the first place,

I don't think I'm wrong,
I have talked to many people,
A lot have talked about their dads,
From I what have heard,
The majority of them have bad experiences,
I don't think these are all coincidences,

What is happiness?
Family, friends, clothing, money,
You can't choose your family,
You can choose your friends,
Who will be closer to you,
Than real family,

If you are a content creator,
You want to look good for her,
Or yourself.
Maybe it is the journey,
Not the destination,
Once your dreams come true,
What will you do?

I think it's the journey,
I mean if you put limits on,
Oh, damn what now,

Well you'll end up like hamster wheel,
It stops working for the hamster,
They have to go without it for a while,
Just like your bubble it grows and grows,
It is inevitable it's going to burst,
Whether it's your last or your first,
Either way make you sure it's fun,
If it isn't cut it off like the top of a champagne bottle,
You can have your dopamine fix driving full throttle.

Rich & Rude

Most people say don't meet your idols,
In real life they aint like the way you think they are,
I mean they can be very rude but they just put a front on for cameras,
I mean some celebrities joke about their career,
There isn't no kindness here,
Just get them another beer,
Let them all cheer,
How long can they be nice for?
If this is the case don't open the door.

What's that you mean to say they are no good on the dancefloor?
Yeah but I've just bought the concert DVD and they looked like a pro,
Whatever they have been like it was all fake,
As fake as their belly with an hourglass figure,
They may be a tiger who is funny like Tigger,
Of course, we know that Tigger isn't real that's exactly my point.

I know this is a cliché that is over used,
However, it is true not everything is as it seems,
We may all breath the same air,
However, that doesn't all is fair,
I mean if you go to Las Vegas,
The humidity is like 80% heat,
20% cool,
I know I've been twice,
Before my life got messed up.
Did you know that WhatsApp originated from the Budweiser advert?
With the frogs said whaaaats upppppp??

You know what they say?
Have a good day,
Sometimes you don't know whether truly mean it,
Then the night time comes and guess what?
They must have meant it because I did have a good day,
A great day in fact.

Are you afraid of people saying it to you?
As for a lot of the time it's not genuine!
Yes, I do like Jess Glynne.

Broke & Kind

Some of the nicest people tend to be broke,
No, they don't ask for money,
That just makes you want to give it to them even more,
You know pride comes before a fall,
That's why you should be generous,
Put your money where your heart is,
It's called showbusiness for a reason,
You have to have a talent to show to become successful,
You have to be hungry for it,
I aint talking a meal,
I'm talking a thrill,

That you love to do,
Your audience loves too,
That is what will get you through,
If you enjoy it,
Then your audience will love it too,

If you look miserable,
Then like a flick of a channel,
They have already tuned out,
They don't want someone to depress you,
They want someone who impresses you,

The truth about this person has such bright blue eyes,
Like if there were a competition; they would win a prize,
For their beauty,
Not only on the outside,
The inside too,

How has this happened to you,
No one seems to know,
You could have been someone's boo,
That is the truth,
So, I hope you have big pockets,
Or perfect hearing,

All they may need,
Is someone to talk to,
That someone could be you,
Here you go,

Go get some lunch,
Forget any insults,
Make them think you can do somersaults,
Say remember what comes around goes around.

Mind

If you have a clear mind,
That opens up the whole world,
For you to be talented and succeed,
Everyone is a human being,
Although, it may not seem that way,
With celebrities who you think were born
With a silver spoon in their mouth,
You feel like they are superior,
Look at the musicians that have become billionaires,
I do believe that took years in the making.

There was no faking,
They're may have been some extra taking,
Like the song hey big spender,
They are tender,
Inside they could have mental health conditions,
However, it may be that helped them,
What these last years have taught me,
That this coronavirus can happen to anyone,
Rich or Poor,
Young or Old,
Celebrities or nobodies,
We are all on the same team,
We all want this pandemic to go,
It just won't,

Not all of it has been bad though,
It has shown that no matter how much money you have,
You can catch it,
No that isn't bat shit,
Covid.19 needs to go away,
People won't be taking their loved ones for granted.

Finally

So after finally ringing nearly every day this week,
Finally, I will be able to go out the next one,
Forget twenty-twenty-one,
It feels like twenty-fifty-one,
Finally, I will be getting a new community carer,
Is it a him or a her,
It is a bloke,
Hopefully I will be with him for years,
I might have a couple of tears of joy,

I haven't even met him yet,
I hope so even though we haven't met,
This is going to be a long weekend,
Halloween and my sister's birthday intertwine,
No, I can no longer drink wine,
Weren't those the days,
Me and mum would pop out,
Get Gallo rose,
Me and mum were like "you have the last glass",
I was like "You bought it you have it",

Okay, fair enough "since you twisted my arm",
I don't mean any harm,
So glad you found your charms,
I hope the new bloke makes me feel safe,
It will be like we are stuck in a time warp,
It will be completely different,
Some may say I have traded in my old life for a new one,
Clapper is no longer working for me,
Only one person misses me,
Good on her, that's what you call a real friend,
I miss her like hell too,
It feels I am in a relationship with her,
This is just the intermission,
We have just changed position,

I got seven-thousand-four-hundred-followers,

All that is left is her,
One friend, one fan, one follower all wrapped into one,
Oh, that's the only one and that's done.

Nothing Lasts Forever

We all know that nothing is forever,
Even friends that have become family,
What about a meaningful relationship with her,
Clapper is behind this made sure I can't gift,
No, I'm not a thrift,
They were all about woodcock,
They couldn't give a damn about my disappearance,
For all they knew, I could have passed away,
I mean being absence for one day,
No need to worry.

However, nine is time to worry,
Everyone is too busy,
This really made me realise,
God can give you money,
That does not bring me happiness,
I haven't been happy for days,
It's the opposite of home and away,
Further apart, more depressed I will become,
It feels like my heart has been turned into stone,

It's not my phone,
It's the apps that are on there,
However, you can't have the apps without the phone,
I was thinking how could you go without social media,
He didn't he just had them on his tablet,
Not the kind you take,
The one you make yours,
When one door closes another one opens,
Without warning,
It feels like I have lost a part of me,
I don't feel free,
No, I don't drink tea,

It's like oh I'll have a sandwich that'll make it better,
I feel like I am going through a breakup by letter,
Choose one thing to replace another,

I got to get on with my family; no, I don't have a brother,
It's temporary this social media,
Do you like him or do you like her?
Why can't I like both?
Too many cooks spoil the broth,
I look funny with the table cloth (on my head),
Yes, I do love the froth,
On my cappuccino,
You aint telling me no,
I will find something else to do,
I didn't need the money,
However, I don't want to be lonely,
So, I'll have the money and the honey,
Baby, you are everything I need,
No, I am not wearing tweed.

Christmas

1 month to go

Have you created a list?
This is a case of where ignorance isn't bliss,
We are standing under mistletoe so give me a kiss,
With a twist let's French kiss like we're in Paris,
Trees decorated with your favourite colour of tinsel,
My electric toothbrush still has working bristles,

I don't need presents that I'm not going to use,
If it was down to me but I know I love Christmas season,
Which starts earlier and earlier each year,
I let out a tear because no present can replace my dad,
I don't have many photos of him not just at Christmas all year long,
However, I remember the memories of us four going on holiday,
Before I got my disability,
I'm lucky that I had so many holidays to look back on,

A lot of people in the U.S.A. haven't been on holiday far away,
I guess it's like working a theme park,
It's cool for the people going on the rides,
But what about the cashiers who just accept the money,
I never thought of it that way before,

Also, what about the people who are tour guides,
Having to say the same things every time,
Every time the public climb upstairs to the top deck of the bus,
You don't have to make much of a fuss,
Just you being here is enough,
A lot of families are broken,
Due to what is going on at the moment.

Best time of the

YEAR

Christmas is known to be the best time of the year,
With a lot of Christmas cheer,
It is because the art of giving,
Never grows old,
Whether you are 9 or 99,
Some people see it as a test,
Forget all of the rest,
Did you make their year?

With the surprise gifts you bought them,
Ignite that smoke in their eyes,
Where they smile so wide,
You can see their crow's feet near each eye,
Even if their smile is hidden,
You can tell they are happy,
Because of this.

It's not about just giving,
It's about giving for what you are receiving,
Now of course you don't know what they got you,
If they don't get it and don't like it too,
You still have each other,
Whether they are your mum, sister, dad, uncle, aunt or nana,
Resolve your differences it's best to be good at this special time of year,
With a cup of good cheer that gives you that warm feeling and lovely
aftertaste.

We all know that when you are grown up,
Some of the magic is no longer there,
It becomes not about the presents,
The presence of your family is good enough,
You all know this if you have ever lost someone,
You will know what I mean,

I used to find it hard to believe in Santa,

As we have a fake fireplace,
That doesn't lead to a chimney,
So how can Santa come down,
When there isn't one,
I mean now I think about it I think we left the garage door,
Open for him to walk through and eat a mince pie and a glass full of brandy,
Which he needed to give him the energy to go from home to home,
Don't worry he didn't forget to say hello to the gnome.

Naughty or Nice

Have you been naughty or nice,
Have you got your list Santa?
Do you like Fanta,
Because it has been sent to ya,
Wait stop right there,
I'm the one that does the giving,
It's my reason for living,
My purpose when I can't think of anything else I'm good at,

Hold on Santa,
It's just a kind gesture,
It was not given to mess with ya,
Oh, jolly good that's good to hear,
Ho, ho, ho,
That burning Christmas pudding,
Needs to be blown out,
In order to be eaten,
By many people not just the one,
Santa has his portion as a treat for delivering presents,
To the nice boys and girls,
The naughty ones only get a lump of coal,
With the tag inscription that says "try to be nice next year",
The naughty children were silently sobbing,
'A lump of coal what a cheek' they thought,

Santa has his reasons,
Remember he reviews you across the year,
Not just on Christmas eve,
Believe it or not,
It's true there's always next year,
Hopefully for you,
Change your ways,
You will get more than presents,
You will become friends with other boys and girls,
Only if you are nice,
Not mean or naughty,

Correct yourself now,
It will be a new beginning,
Your baubles will be hanging and shimmering on your Christmas tree,
All by you turning the tree on at the wall,

You don't have to be over six-foot-tall,

Nice boys and girls got to go see the making of Harry Potter,
In Watford as a treat for being so well behaved all year,
'It's amazing here' one of the boys said,
'I want to be sorted by the sorting hat' one of the girls asked,
'You are very intriguing, very clever and loyal' you belong to RAVENCLAW.
'I always wondered what house I would be in' the girl said.
'Thank god, it wasn't Slytherin!' she added.

We went on the famous HOGWARTS EXPRESS a lot of the boys and girls said
at the same time,
This is exactly how it was in the movies,
Doing all this made me hungry, I have the munchies,
No, I haven't done any drugs I'm just very excited,
It's better than I ever imagined.

They all told their teacher,
Oh, thank you so much without you and Santa this would've have been
possible,
The feels and the vibe were magical it felt like I could have been a student
there,
I know it's not real but boy if it was I would be the first one to move in to
Hogwarts.

Roll back to Reality

Winning on the lottery,
Is tax free without doubt,
Make them guess I won a lot,
From the machines that are owned by Camelot.

Am I the only one that remembers their used to be a Guinevere,
There is no longer one called Guinevere,
Over here,
I wonder whose decision that was,
Guinevere can't survive without Camelot,
Camelot can survive without her though
All of the draws that Camelot has played,
Not hurt by the absence of what Guinevere could have made.

Even the national lottery company can't believe no one is winning the jackpot,
So now when there is a rolldown players don't just get a free shot,
They get a fiver too which is added to their pot.
Was it a coincidence they only introduced it?
Since I have been playing the lotto,
They still have the same motto.

Just like TESCO has always had the same motto,
They are the only supermarket to keep their slogan; to keep to their original saying,
It seems to be a winning battle as it still is paying off,
Just like a preppy snooty student at Eton.
TESCO is still the leading supermarket selling baby back ribs with a lot of meat on.

I Will Get There

One of my friends on TikTok,
They said you need a thousand followers to go live on the clock,
I go on live I don't get many viewers however I get no trolls,
Mum couldn't get the sausage rolls,
I ain't talking about the small ones,
If you are going to do a job don't do it half done.

I have over twenty-six seven thousand followers,
On my main account and over six thousand on my 2nd account,
Right in the centre of the capital city of the UK,
Are you okay? Tomorrow is what you make it,
So, pretend you are celebrating the song you wrote is a massive number one hit.

Repeat this mantra,
I am good enough,
Inhale then exhale,
You will survive to tell the tale

* * * * * * * * * * * * * * * * * *

In the upcoming week,
I hope that I survive after the covid vaccine,
However, this new version of me,
I want to keep just like everyone knows I don't like a cup of tea.
TikTok thinks I'm American,
I'll do what I can,
Just like Jackie Chan,
Or Anthony Joshua,
Everyone loves their ma,
After someone makes you a drink you should say ta!
If I don't survive until next week,
At least I know I did what I could,
Like everyone else has and would,
You can have your own pud,
Knowing you did what you should.
I will get there,
Forget people who stare,
We have taken the vaccine,
To put an end to this pandemic,
So, people can still go out there and kick,
It's like the lottery games,

There are lions that need to be tame,
Which are the devils of temptation,
That grab thirty million pounds from our pockets,
For every game that is played and lost.

Only a fraction of people wins,
It's like what it says a lottery,
There will be a lot who lose,
It's all what you do and what you choose.

I am going to do my numbers for next Saturday,
It's like my smartphone is low on battery,
Will it last or will it die if you film videos in the same category!

Dad And I

Although in my early teens I didn't have much of a father-son relationship,
Release any stress and try to be the best even though I wasn't that tall,
I was playing Tiger Woods PGA Tour on PS2 with my dad,
We bonded over golf, how hard it was in real life yet so easy on the video game so I wasn't that bad.

I remember getting a 59 for 18 holes on the video game,
My dad said no one has ever got this in a real life round,
Dad was proud of me which most of the time I thought he thought I was lame,
My mum kept on going on about people that are good in real life not just the game,
They got fame from becoming being good at golf I was thinking 'ignore this shame'

So, we went from PS2 game to watching Golf on the TV,
Of course, it was on the BBC,
I could cry a sea for both my dad and peter alliss,
My dad's lifetime clock was up,
Then last year Peter alliss died I was so upset,
I didn't need to meet him you could just tell he was a good man.

The commentary team on the BBC was really good,
When compared to SKY coverage it did stand
Up against the commentators are what make it great,
It was live on the weekend on BBC so they could only do it on take.

We watched golf on holiday too,
They had some of the British channels,
No, we didn't need a manual,
We were in Portugal I don't think it was in Portuguese,
So, we were pleased.

How Quick Does Karma Work

If I have just had an argument with someone,
They were in the wrong,
Just listening to a song,
How quickly do they get what I call 'Instant Karma'?
We aint talking about the Dalia Llama.

What I define as 'Instant Karma' is,
Something bad happen to them five to ten minutes passed the point of taking
the piss,
Like being two minutes late for the bus home,
After they have just had a moan,
(About something trivial),

When good karma is entitled to the right person,
How long does it take for that good karma to manifest?
Why does it feel like some days all there is bad karma?
When all you have been is a charmer.

When is it too early to celebrate a bit of good karma before it turns into bad
karma.

They say don't live in the past,
When will we look back at these times saying remember when we had to wear
masks,

They say in the present,
However, if u have deadlines to meet,
How can u know whether you can take the heat?
Get out of the kitchen,
Going to a restaurant that has 3 Michelin(star)

Who?

I think mum wants me,
However, I don't think dad did,
He always had a stone cold look on his face,
Like he ate something that gave him a bad aftertaste,
This may be true he had a look at me that you could not decipher,
Even without her.

If anything was true,
It would be that dad in my early teens,
He was there in spirit but his soul was not as he was mean,
It was like he was not keen,
On being a father to two children,
Just one like china and their one child policy,
He probably listened to Morrissey,
Like the illusion of wizard of Oz and Dorothy.

Dad was never really there,
When he was alive,
Didn't show any affection,
If we were both on Twitter,
I wouldn't have received a single mention.

I went to go to detention,
I knocked on the door,
I was looking at the floor,
While waiting for the teacher to open their room,
The only sound was the caretaker sweeping up the dirt with their broom.

They never opened their door.
What for? I hadn't done anything wrong,
Only realised that I was telling the truth through song.

TikTok to Clapper

I didn't realise how quickly people could ditch TikTok,
They went over to Clapper like the changing of the clock,
It was like TikTok was just there to get mocked,
Like an undercooked apple crumble,
Anyone who had their money in TikTok would take a tumble.

However, I have seen the Clapper Live,
Only the duo live version,
Diversion from watching the Single show,
I try to do the single live but no one joins,
It felt like a kick in the groin,
I don't think you can get banned,
If you can you must have to do something really bad.
It would feel like someone was taking your teddy bear away,
Which would ruin your day.

I joined Clapper last October,
Now it's only kicking off in March,
This is a bit harsh,
They only tell you about the clapper verification,
This month so that was sneaky of them,
Like a woman's skirt split through the hem.

Why?

Why I am not getting the success others are getting,
No, I am not messing,
Where is my blessing and how long will I have to wait for it?
I have had enough of my TikTok views being s***,
What everyone wants to know is how do you get that blue tick!

Why, oh, why does this happen,
It's like seeing the same pattern,
Every day, I sit down I don't have a crown,
Why send me a brown crystal flower,
If you are going to send a flower make sure it gives me flower power.

It's happy hour but I can't drink,
What annoying thing to think,
Not even a cosmopolitan,
I don't even know why I am tolerant,
What benefit is there from them,
Getting drunk for a few hours to forget my reality,
Maybe things will get better after I give to charity.

Jolly Good Time

It will only be a jolly good time spent,
Over the Christmas period,
If everyone I love is happy,
Smiling from ear to ear,
Let's all have a jolly good time,
Santa is going to be rewarding us,
More than ever this year,

After all, to say it's been a challenging year,
Is an understatement, the understatement of the decade?
Just thinking about it is giving me a bad headache,
Too bad to medicate,
At the moment,
Let's make the most of this upcoming Christmas,
As it's going to be a very cold winter starting from December,
ALL the way through to the end of February,

Whatever mother nature throws at us,
We won't let it get us,
Down whatever happens,
We will not be the toadstools super Mario flattens,
If we are knocked down we will keep getting up,
Again, and again just like rocky when we rise will muster all strength,
No matter the length of the battle,
They will be running away like cattle,
We light a candle for them,
They need it, whereas we don't,

If it isn't a jolly good time,
We will make it one,
We will cherish every chime big ben makes,
Every cake each baker bakes,
Every bumper tv-guide that tells you the fortnight before Christmas schedules
and afterwards,
The schedules into the new year!

Jolly good time,

Santa will be there to deliver anything materialistic,
The thing I want is not materialistic,
I want us all to get on as a family of three,
Including my mum, my sister and me,

Wasn't it funny when one of my friends has a sister just like mine,
I knew he wasn't like that in real life, TikTok doesn't work that way though,
That is why he didn't get on there,
They had cotton wool balls over their eyes when it come to him,
He isn't even called Tim.

Don't You Eat That

I heard that they eat reindeer,
Made me feel sick,
Not precious reindeer,
I swear they are nearly extinct,
So, don't bring them to the brink,
I can't believe it,
The reindeer should be protected,
Why aren't they?
There are a lot of turkeys,
Who do you hear saying that?
They eaten reindeer,
No one but these sick people,
What if some kid found this out,

They would be distraught,
I thought it was bad when they were eating horse,
Now it's reindeer,
Do they actually know its reindeer though?
People eating horse meat didn't know they eating it,
So fair play to them,
People know its reindeer though,
They are just eating it like it's normal,
Like chicken,
Where do these people come from?
Anyone who has kids have to try and shield their children's eyes and ears,

People eat deer but never reindeers I thought,
I know they eat weird things in the jungle,
This never came to my mind though,
I guess it is probably like offal,
I would never eat that either,
Especially sheep brains,
All blended together,
Yuck, yuck, yuck.

Happy Easter

A second Easter in a pandemic,
I ain't even talking bull****,
I wish I was,
Like some people who couldn't give a toss,
These are usually people that are a boss.

E is for Easter,
Take care of her,
Especially in the pool's cold water,
Is this what Americans' call the spring break,
I've had nearly as much as I can take.

Happiness is made from your decisions,
You should not need permission,
Have you got a packet of tissues in your pocket?
You will need them if you sneeze ready for it.

I can't believe it I have had not a single crème egg,
Its Prince Harry and Meghan's first Easter away,
While the rest of the royals stay,
The great-grandchildren note their great-granny on money,
They were told that she was on all legal tender, all money.

Want

Why do we want things?
We are human beings,
People tease us with it,
We think it's taken so long we don't give a s***.

We all need that dopamine hit,
Like wanting to know how to do that magic trick,
Who is it they call mickey blue eyes?
Frank Sinatra is who and who is mickey,
Other than the obvious one who is mickey mouse,
That might visit you stay in the hotel,
Oh, don't forget Minnie,
Mum finally admits I was skinny.

Stop this bulls*** if I ask for an honest opinion,
You should give a blunt honest one,
Others may want one that is sugar-coated,
Which other remarks are.

I HAVE more THAN 9 Lives

I have had at least 9 near-death experiences,
No, they are not coincidences,
The black bloke in Final Destination,
Has some explaining to do,
I have cheated death so much I've lost count,
It has skipped me and went on to another,
No, I do NOT have a brother,
I love my mother.

Do you believe in guardian angels?
Maybe I am one for someone,
Last time I went to the neurological hospital,
I saw how thick the file was so big to see,
It would take weeks maybe a month to read it and he has documentation all on me.

I watch Top Gear,
However, I don't know why some cars have 5 gears and others have seven,
If I drove I would do zero to eleven,
And see how much it would take to do that extra speed limit.

I know I should go to sleep,
However, I need a few hours to wind down,
In this place we call a town,
I have finally got over my phobia of a clown,
I have developed a new phobia though of drowning in the bath,
Since watching thirteen reasons why,
Don't be shy it's only water,
Except it wasn't it was five pints of blood,
Don't step in that mud.

Dry

It's been so long,
No one has been my girlfriend,
I haven't had a spend,
Which is bound to change,
What is my age,
I am full of rage.

I got courage,
Sex is my leverage,
As I'm turning the page,
Cage fighting is on the tv,
This should be easy,
I close my eyes,
As they trim my fringe,
I get a tinge,
Down there I feel,
No, I'm not ill,
Waiting for them to open the till.

If only I could get COD BLACK OPS four,
Working apparently there is too much to store,
I fancied killing some zombies,
It ain't even Monday,
I don't need to drive,
In order to thrive.

Limo with heated seats,
Keep us warm while we are reading Keats,
No video games with cheats,
I want meat like sirloin steak,
Does that give you another reason to hate?
You keep hating, while I keep taking up your mind,
What's happened to your life,
Hating has consumed you,
While I aint nowhere near to feeling blue,
Is your energy taken up?
Fill up my cup.

Money

Ain't it funny,
We are all earning money,
At home like good people,
We don't have covid we are cheerful,
Far from being tearful.

Cheers to another day,
Waiting until the end of lockdown,
And it ain't even x factor,
Women using max factor,
While a man is out driving a tractor,
This quiz is hard and it ain't even the krypton factor.

Everything is money,
So, don't spend it all at once,
Unless you're a dunce,
Health is money,
Honey,
Mental Health is money,
So, don't come off of the meds,
The doctor said.
Time is money,
That you can't get back,
Especially if you have heart attack.
Don't be stupid and push your body to the max.
You don't want there to be a tax.

Right Day, Wrong Time

So, I treated myself,
I thought I needed no help,
Turns out I was wrong,
I ain't even called john,
We pick the chicken kebabs up with metal prongs.

We aren't even in Hong Kong,
What is taking so long,
Them trolls are just mongs,
They don't deserve their place in this song.

I need to curb my gambling,
It ain't even worth it,
Everything in moderation,
You need to know your diction,
Even though you got a triple distinction.

People thinking that people on social media,
Don't have an education are wrong,
I have a first class (honour's) degree in computing,
I didn't even do media studies,
I learnt it all on my own,
So goodbye to the haters,
A lot of entrenpreurs don't even finish their degree,
So, you forget about them hateful comments,
I don't even have to do social media,
I do because I enjoy it thoroughly,

If you ain't getting trolls,
Maybe you need some more toilet rolls,
Is it all taking over and have you lost control?
No, why did you end your live,
I don't even have sour cream and chive,

Crisps and my dad weren't even called clive.

Summer Weather, Spring Time (SW:ST)

Spring is here,
Keep loved ones near,
COVID.19 is what we all fear
So, we just let out a tear.

When they say have you drunk 2 litres of water,
Do tears count because then I might nearly be there,
Some days can be such a mare,
No, it wasn't in the night,
It was in the day,
Hence mare,
Here is a newspaper to tear.

Who is actually sticking to the two-metre distance,
Have you missed any of your loved ones?
Replaced human interaction with games,
I know it is lame,
I am going to review the limits,
Gambling is like a venus flytrap,
It will eat and eat until there is nothing left.

It doesn't care how little you have,
You can spend more money,
This ain't honey that never goes off,
No point showing off if you don't have the funds,
Are you okay Hun?
What would you do if I wasn't?
Just choose to not continue the convo,
Even if you were about to eat the last rolo.

Mother's Day

We all love our mums,
Even if they have a tum,
They let out a hum,
When they see their present,
You got them they were not hesitant.

Our mums are like don't get me anything,
They love it when you ignore them,
And get them a present anyway,
Like a bouquet of flowers,
Which will give them joy for hours,
Days if they treat them right,
The unspoken rule is don't get them the same thing twice,
Some mums don't know what to do with a gift card

They are so focused on making sure everyone else has what they need,
So that's not a good idea,
Maybe something from the heart,
It's best to get something that you know they will like from the start,
That would be something that would be smart.

Finish the day off with her favourite bottle of wine,
Also watch whatever she wants it's her day,
So, let her spend it her way,
Of course, including you and her other loved ones.

Christmas Nostalgia

Thinking back to Christmas when you were younger,
I used to go to sleep before midnight on Christmas day,
As I was told Santa wouldn't come if I stayed up past midnight on Christmas eve night,
Of course, this was when I believed in Santa Claus,
He ain't just any fat bloke with white hair and a big belly and beard,
Where did Santa get the money for all of the presents in the world,
Santa was delivering the kids presents made by the elves,
While they are sleeping and dreaming of their Christmas wish list,

The elves were all short and fat in Lapland waiting for Santa's instructions,
They can function on their own but they need prompting to get it right,
On the weekends they work day and nights,
They don't want to go and take flights,
So, this is why Santa has his seven reindeers including Rudolph,
Rudolph is special as he has a red nose,
He always gets to choose where to sit,
The reindeer at the back,
Has to share the space with the presents,
No presents can fall off the flying sleigh,
Especially if they are on the nice list,

This is where ignorance isn't bliss,
Mrs. Claus kisses Santa Claus on the lips,
Santa is everyone's stan,
Santa's the man with the plan,
The gifts are given to him,
Santa needed to not confuse them,
With each other,
With one another.

I used to wake up on Christmas day at like 3am,
Demanding I open presents there and then,
It was the highlight of the year,
If you were born in the late eighties,
In the nighties I was like one to ten,
We used to have really big Christmas stockings,
They died out after about ten years,

That left me in a pool of my own tears.

Christmas Present
& Future

A lot of adults who love the festive season still have Christmas stockings,
It depends on the family and I guess how well off they are,
I used to get to terry's chocolate orange which as I a kid was impossible crack open,
It felt like fort Knox,
Why did they stop,
When everyone else still had their Christmas stockings?
With Christmas stockings comes Christmas stocking fillers,
I never wrote a list for the Christmas stocking,
Every year it was a surprise,
So that's why it wasn't as bad as every year it was different,
That's how it would stay,
It felt like it each year one thing was taken away,
I had a Cadbury selection box,
That soon stopped,

Now I'm older I get my own advent calendar,
Most of the time the chocolate ones were Cadbury's,
I would experiment some years and the chocolate weren't as good,
You never know until you try it, chocolate is chocolate right?
Wrong! Some cheap chocolate tastes horrible,
It was definitely worth paying the extra for the better flavour,
Don't worry you will thank me later,
No need to be a hater.

Waiter or waitress?
Neither, they have been replaced by screens.
If it is like this in twenty-twenty-one,
What will it be like in twenty-thirty-one,
People wonder where the bacteria comes from,
People going to the toilet and not washing their hands,
Especially when they go a number two,
However, who is monitoring who?

Another job made redundant,
Bang goes their grant to help with their degree,
Nothing is free any more,

If you don't like it there's the door,
Actually, I need the money even if the job feels like a chore,
The janitor makes some money and some money is better than no money,
It's wrong what they say more' money more' problems,
Without money you couldn't get anything,
That is why everyone is always like I need payday to come sooner and sooner,
Each month, month and month after month.

Christmas Ties

It's that time of the year once again,
Where you are supposed act like ten,
If I go to sleep before Christmas night,
The last thing you want is an argument on Christmas eve,
You just want to believe,
That the Christmas feels are in the air,
It is in the air when you hear them familiar,
Jingles and bells ringing in the church,
You watch midnight mass,
Once the clock struck midnight,
You welcome in yet another Christmas,
You have made it to yet another one,
I have got everything I need,
If I have my family spending their time with me,

My aunts come around on Christmas day,
Bringing their kids who are my cousins,
That is at least twelve people,
With close family that's fifthteen,
We get the Christmas dining table all pristine,
The turkey and vegetables are cooking it's going to be a big feast,
For all of us to each dig in; I go to eat the turkey first as that's the best meat,

The Christmas decorations make it that little extra special,
We all gather around the tv to watch top of the pops and see who got the
Christmas number one for this year and of course who got the number one
Christmas album of this year.

Christmas ties every family together,
Celebrities reunite with each other member,
This is the magic of Christmas and what it does,
Santa has a big white beard with white facial hair fuzz,
I'm like YAY new Christmas presents but it all means nothing,
If my family are not together with me and I aint bluffing,

Christmas was all about the presents when I was younger,
Not anymore, I mean I can buy what I want if I save up,

So, make me a gingerbread latte and put it in my cup,
I was so desperate for the coffee I got a hiccup,
Don't forget me I'm just like the gingerbread latte coming up hot,
Take your shot of expresso,
It's like a shot of coffee with a very high amount of caffeine,
When I say it, I mean it so it's like five coffees in one.

We will have a turkey this year,
If you want you can have a beer,
To celebrate the festive cheer,
It's Christmas here,
Put away our differences,
You know what Christmas is really about,
All sitting down together at the dinner table,
Being able to be happy,
Happy as Larry,
With your close family,
Of course, I won't forget my fanily,
Fans and Family make my fanily,

All of these people are trying to be funny,
By drinking corona beer,
While we're still in the middle of corona virus pandemic,
They are taking the mick,
Until tragedy strikes.

CORONA
CHRISTMAS

Corona is here,
Something that we all fear,
So is it completely normal to shed a tear,
Is it becoming too much to bare?

What tier are you in?
Them tickets for a weekend getaway,
Are no longer worth it if you want to survive this day,
Even if the weather was like may.

Multi-millionaires are in their own league,
Their power to change the law,
They say money can't buy you happiness,
No stress for the millionaires you can guess,

Will the celebrity bat an eyelash when something is wrong?
No, they won't as money can get them out of nearly anything,
Or is this just the beginning of a two-sided face of the law,
Money is not a problem for them as they have it in abundance.

It's okay the fine didn't even make a dent in their savings,
It's like they are bathing in money,
Also, what is their money like?
These celebrities bank balances are full of honey,
It never goes off,
It never goes away,
When it does start to dwindle,
Don't worry they're go on chat shows,
Quiz shows, competition announcements in which thousands or millions have
a go.

Darling If I Don't Wake Up

If I don't wake up,
I have gone into a peaceful sleep,
Which is cheap,
I won't be a burden anymore to you,
It will just be you two.

You don't have to do give me a fancy funeral,
If you do give me a funeral use my savings,
Don't worry about my beard or hair that need trimming,
No need to change my clothes.

Mum sorry for doing this,
At least you won't have me nagging you,
I feel so blue,
Which is ironic,
As that is my favourite colour,
No need to dust down my bedroom,
With a broom or mobile vacuum,
It won't matter soon,
Just like whether it's a half or full moon.

My sister is going to ace her new job,
She will finally stay there,
You can have my teddy bear,
As a memento from me,
You can finally work the whole week at home,
Now you are mum's only child,
You'll get little to mild problems,
So, was I the scapegoat?
Or did you just make that up,
Was the boat big for both of us,
Or just for you,
So, I drown and you can have mum to yourself,
Just think of me as a book on my bookshelf,
Every story has its end,
So, don't depend,

On me surviving this storm,
The air is cold,
Maybe I'll get ill.
My sister will see it as a thrill.
Sorry about the drill dad couldn't get.
I am going into a long sleep,
You don't have to sweep.

See you later,
I know the haters will probably have a party,
No, I am not Marty,
I can't go to the future,
I guess this is it,
I must go now.

Smartphone or Smart Gadget

Should they be called smartphones,
When smartphones aren't used to call,
They are used to do everything else but that,
Have you got very long hair you hide with a hat,
Does the length of your hair make you lazy?
Well no we are in the middle of a pandemic if you are able-bodied then maybe.

I couldn't believe it,
I did a TikTok live and received no trolls spouting their s***,
I think the title of the live probably was why,
I said prize draw live they are not stupid they are like hi!

Okay I should try and go live more,
But when trolls come knocking I start looking for the door,
Apparently if someone is a troll to you and you block,
They may have multiple accounts and their friends might come for you,
So, I was thinking the moment will pass however this isn't class where there is a teacher,
You need to have your moderator,
To do their job and block the ones that are hating ya!

You didn't build up your account,
To get it shut down,
Just let them be a clown,
Watch them drown,
Don't worry they don't live in your town.

If they do live close,
Try to bear them at the most,
Because you don't know how near,
Definitely don't block them dear,
If they say clearly where they are,
The anxiety starts to take over,
They even have a range rover,
One of the biggest cars on the market,
You know what is their target.

Success at University/College

You may be thinking something obvious,
But being a novice will help you in the long run,
Don't own a smartphone otherwise that studying just aint going to get done,
You are likely saying to your parents I'll study at one,
There are loads of distractions and you need to act,
They are taking up traction in your mind,
On one hand they want to be the parent that is kind,
But on the other hand; they want you to be a pupil that will shine,
No, I will do what I want I am fine they say,
Today is a new day,
You are fine now but what happens on results day,
Will your parents say don't worry or kick you out?
This aint about clout,
Did I just get messed about her parents thought?

Why? Secretly their child got their hands on a smartphone,
Eighty percent of her time was taken up with it,
Why did we just pay tuition fees?
Well for her to be on the smartphone,
This deserves a moan,
Not even by a trombone by a dad who had a monotone voice,
He says she had one decision to study,
They didn't even make a story like I need to have a study buddy.

Quality

It aint about the quantity,
It's all about the quality,
If they said you could have five moments,
Instead of one meaningful moment,
I would choose the one,
Like the new format of these poems,
They may be shorter,
However, they are more meaningful,
Like when you think of a glass half full or empty,
What do you think? I Think of it as half full,
That's like saying is this person are half tall,
Or half short,
Half short just sounds weird.

Sometimes weird is best,
Other times the rest is better,
It was good to meet her,
Yes, I have man fur,
Would you defer?
Me or do you like men with no hair like ken,
"No, I don't like ken" She says,
"Oh good" I reply,
No that's not a lie,

No point dressing up,
In a suit and tie,
That is not me,
That would be fake,
As fake as the icing on that cake,

Make a good first impression,
I would say have a shave,
Impress them like Maeve,
You don't get a second chance,
At a first impression.

I mean if I think about it we didn't start off well,
With her having the range rover which ran over me,
So, there were pros and cons to the previous community carer,
I tend to talk a lot if I'm nervous it feels up the space,
Like an airbag would,

I hope it goes swimmingly,
Whatever will be will be,
Which is ironic as I can't swim,
Just have high hopes that I like him.

Hour by Hour

Hour by hour,
The time passes by,
Like a pumpkin pie,
I was in such pain earlier I felt like I was going to die,
However, the feeling passed,
Now I feel like the phantom,
Look where he come from,
Now he aint called Tom,
I reply as I chomp, chomp on chocolate,
I know I am more fortunate,
Than some but that is because I have been shrewd,
I had been brought up like I was Martin's Lewis' child,

I have had a mild mentality,
Like a nobody,
Not told anybody anything,

Hour by Hour,
As each second,
Each minute,
Each hour,
Each day,
Passes I make sure I make the most of it,
As every second, minute, hour, day,
Counts like it was my last one,
Done, done, done and done,

It's all about having some fun,
Otherwise you would be dumb,
Make that your rule of thumb,
Hum, hum, hum, hum,
You gotta love your family,
Especially your parents,
They are worth more than liquid gold,
As your life unfolds,
You're going to need your sibling/s,
So, remember love brother/s or sister/s,

Hour by Hour,
Sometimes the time seems to go slow,
However, once the time has gone,

There's no way of getting it back,
So, don't fight and don't go to sleep after argument,
You just don't know what will happen,
You will regret it and there's no going back,
That's exactly what happened to my mum and sister,
The memories of rage and anger,
Were the last memories they have of my father,

It all fits into place,
Why they didn't want to do a eulogy,
I did one though as he didn't shout at me,
The last memory I have of him is creating a pumpkin pie,
I had helped prepare it with my father,
Which was a happy memory,
That I can recite,
With delight.

Hour by Hour,
Second by Second,
Minute by Minute,
Make sure they are all present to you,
Treat every single one as your last ones,
While you are sipping on that cinnamon latte,

Every second by second to hour by hour,
Make sure they are not sour,
Like pure lemon juice,
Just like deuce.

I was going to say what didn't help,
Was Dad had McDonalds twice in the week,
However, I go into a live on Clapper,
This woman said "I've had McDonalds four times this week",
Now she didn't know this about dad,
It was just a coincidence,
Maybe my dads' heart was too weak to carry on,
They say Keep Calm & Carry On,

If you knew my dad,
He wasn't calm all the time,
Just a small thing could set him off,
Like a microwave having a countdown timer,
That's what my dad's temper was like,
Don't get me wrong we had such good times with him,
That last year before he died really mucked him up,

I got my disability and I think it was killing him inside,

He thought it was his fault,
Like a cup of malt.

Joy

Mum is like 'God wouldn't give you anything you couldn't handle',
Oh really? Are you sure that isn't Satan?
That seems pretty blatant of him,
Just how the water can go from 0c to 100c boiling point,
Except it wasn't water it was my muscles going into spasms,
In my lower back and arms,
I'm pretty sure that any pain that I get is from Satan.

What is the happiness hormone?
 Oxytocin or Dopamine,
 I heard it was Oxytocin,
 I aint sure though,

What I do know though,
Cortisol is the stress hormone,
It seems to occur in the morning,
As a warning,
Are you going to make it a good or a bad day?
All I know is what is happening now and the rest of today,
I see you both as my baby,
So, it's a definitely maybe,

In order to have a good day,
Is to have high oxytocin or dopamine levels,
Higher levels of them hormones than cortisol,
It's like building a massive Jenga,
For cortisol to just know it down,
That is what is making frown,

I saw the looks people were giving me when I went out,
They aint what I'm about,
I heard them say while looking at me "he is disturbing",
I had done nothing to them they just wanted to insult,
Me like I was public enemy number one,
I mean I could easily insult her but I aint that childish,
Just wish she gets stung by a jellyfish.

LOL at the title,
It was supposed to be about Joy,
I have talked oxytocin,
Mum thinks me playing the wheel,
Was to try and win money,

It wasn't, it was honey,
I had the money,
I just wanted some fun,
It would give me adrenaline,
Before the melatonin,
Kicked in,
Silence is golden,
Like the leaves turn gold,
During the autumn,
I love the name autumn,
For a girl or a woman.

I loved Autumn in the O.C.
The woman not the season,
I was breathing,

What was the love hormone?
No, I'm not a Mormon,
That's cool man,

If a certain someone thinks,
They will knock another certain someone,
Of the top spot they are kidding themselves.

Both of them are friends but when it comes to the number one spot,
They are all for themselves like I am in a PK battle,
Like a shepherd trying to order all of the cattle,
Into the pen,
Not the biro kind,
Keep that in mind.

One on One

One on one,
They battle to be the top,
What would you buy?
An album you already knew?
Or a completely new one?

I know what I would choose,
Both of them,
However not on CD,
On a streaming service,
I would have bought it on CD,
About five years ago,
Not in this decade though,
I wonder who would win,
Stormzy or Ed Sheeran?

That aint who I am talking about though,
Haven't they both got enough dough,
I aint talking cookie dough,
I would blow a kiss to all of the girls,
Watch them do a twirl,
Not the chocolate bar,
Hahahaha,

One on One,
Can turn friends into enemies,
Or frenemies,
Oh, I wish you good luck,
wink, wink
They aint wishing you that,
I'm ~~sorry~~ not sorry it's my time,
I'll be hitting up the top spot worldwide,
I'll be collecting that brit next year,
For global achievement,
So, I'll wave to you in the distance,
Take your stance,
I aint talking balance,
I'm talking talent.

Six Weeks

After schools broke up in July,
It was time to have to six weeks off,
Go away moth,
I'd rather have a conversation with toff,
In Chelsea while I haven't seen a full episode of
Made in Chelsea,
They all sound posh,
They have a lot of dosh.

Some of them are hot,
Are they too hot to trot?
They definitely don't have a lot of a plot,
They may like regular trips to Harrods,
Not at the moment though because lots of covid,
Sorry for being morbid,
Better than being tall and thick,
I ain't talking about a large milkshake,
What's that? Your arm is sore from the covid vaccine!

I am not being mean I was just being keen,
Well your body language was giving it away,
So be careful with your body language as you give away more than you realise,
If your voice sounds fine but your arms crossed,
You're being defensive,
As well as being pensive.

Apparently if you answer a question,
And you look to the left,
You are telling a porky,
And you are being naughty.

Personal

Do blackboards still exist?
If not while did they feature so long,
Do you wear a thong?
Is this a coincidence?
Did you eat minced beef?
How are your teeth?
Do you have a brief?

Since Kansas City chiefs,
Appeared in the super bowl,
Have you checked your moles?
Do you like to play bowls?
After what Cancer Research UK have told,
You are told one in two will get it,
Or is this a load of bull****.

Some people may call it propaganda,
No, I'm not called Amanda,
Maybe you need to love more Pandas.
Cold Turkey,

If you want something,
I ain't talking about a muffin,
Yes, everyone wants loving,
From your mum, sister or brother,
Girlfriends or boyfriends come and go,
Family is forever where you don't have to put on a show,
Precious moments like blowing out the candles on your birthday cake,
With a brand-new wish to make.

They say can you just quit your bad habits,
Like stop taking your tablets,
No, you can't but you can quit gambling your money,
Honey I can decrease my limits,
It's like this; I can trim my beard,
However, it will go back,
This doesn't mean I need to increase my limits again,
It's a vicious circle, you gamble on the games,
What is lame is you win but then it's not enough,

Because you want to keep winning,
It's like trying to swim in the deep end,
You know you can't you catch yourself drown while you go and pretend.

You wish you could have an out-of-body-experience,
At your own funeral to see whether it's a coincidence,
How many people are there?
I don't want to give myself a scare!
I know my sister wants no one to come,
Maybe she is waiting to be proven right,
Words like that hurt like a knife and keep me up at night,
From the darkest hour comes the brightest light.

Worth A Shot

You can earn a thousand pounds,
Before being taxed on it,
If your business becomes a hit,
You have to submit your tax return,
From what you earn,
Everyone has to do it,
Every little bit,
Look beyond the money,
Are you enjoying yourself,
Is it helping your financial health?

Happiness or Wealth,
If you have to choose one,
What is better,
Happiness of course,
I would feel real remorse,
If I had to choose wealth.
Your health is your wealth,
Your happiness is what you make it.

Don't let your life pass you by,
Also, don't change and ignore people you once called your friends,
Just keep practising zen.

Full Circle

Is it a ghost or a spirit?
I ask 'cos spirits can be good or bad,
However, the ghost can linger in the house,
Like a dead woman's blouse,
Mum said don't dabble in that witches' magic,
Or you could end up conjuring up something tragic,
You might need someone who is a clergyman,
To rid the house of a ghost,
Who could become a host,
Host of one of you in this house,
You may need an exorcist,
To prove the ghost exists,
That definitely aint God who put the ghost there,
It was Satan,

Is one of us the host of two ghosts,
Like Jekyll and Hyde,
Sometimes Jekyll is here,
Other times Hyde is near,

I know mum says "we were told the house wasn't haunted",
However, what about Dad? Is he haunting this house,
I only feel peace at night time,
My sister takes control of the house in the day time,

Was it haunted already?
Can they get in trouble?
If they lie while selling you this house?
When it is!

I've seen enough episodes of supernatural,
That show that you got to burn bones
To get rid of any ghosts or spirits,

It's full circle back to twenty-nineteen,
When there was no TikTok or Clapper,
As they are not working as they should,
Forget the dollars, I want to chat to my friends,
I aint on there to make money
I'm on there to make family.

Unwind

Instead of voicing my opinion about my life,
Over radio for an hour it wasn't even my live,
Yet I dominated it because this man is now cool & kind,
Since the Big Bang Theory made nerdy and clever blokes,
Cool we may not have been without it and I don't mean the weather,
It was about time to spill some of my lucky charms and I aint talkin'
breakfast cereal,
 The gypsy woman was around I gave her fifty-pence or a pound for a lucky
pink heather,
It sudden felt all surreal mum used to drag me to the gypsy woman,
Suddenly when I saw the gypsy woman in my wheelchair I insisted my
community carer to talk to her,

What was good she didn't treat me any different even though I was in my
wheelchair,
It wasn't a nightmare when I met her while in the wheelchair,

I got given two gem stones years and years ago,
The two stones gave what some people could csll good luck for many years,
Although at that time it was time to get a round in I don't drink beers,
Actually, I no longer drink alcohol because of the interaction with medication,

What did marge from The Simpsons say?
Slow and steady wins the race,
Who would win doesn't matter,
People can tell whether you are putting on a front,
So, keep being yourself and stop trying to please everyone,
Do you think Elon Musk and Jeff Bezos are friends?
No way, when it comes to money they both seem to go their separate ways,
Is this how it would stay?
It's a state of play,
Every man or woman for themselves,
Far from teenager working that Saturday job,
Could they fit in a weekend of part-time work?
While still focusing their next idea to get rich,
Getting rid of an itch you have to itch it,
Until it goes, it goes away,
You have to admit that sometimes you just have to ask for help,
You want to believe you can do anything you put your mind too,

However, that maybe true, when the red arrows fly across the sky,
They don't go one after another they all go all the same time,

At the end of the day,
You don't go into work working a cubicle in an office,
To be told here's today's pay,
Do you want it now or at the end of the day?
If they were given today's pay at the start,
There's no motivation for the office work you usually do,
Why did you give me that option?
Now I don't know how to function.

I know I'm not a machine,
I'm not like MR sheen,
Where it's all fresh and clean,
However, below it is crumbling at the seams,

No one is perfect,
This is why people need to be told you're enough,
You're better than enough,
There will be obstacles in the way,
If you could defeat them you get the pay.

Some people just seem to stop right before they succeed,
Others may train themselves into new skills like kneed,
Kneading the dough into some brand-new baked loaves of bread,
What does it say in the lord's prayer say,
Give us this, our daily bread,
Guild ourselves away from temptation.

Don't say I'll just have a flutter on roulette,
If it lands on your number you get ten-times on that number,
Why such a big pay-out, it is all for clout,
What did they do to the lotto,
Add ten numbers and change their motto,
The national lottery is a business,
A company, what does a company need to survive,
Profit, so if it rolls over they have accepted all of those bets,
Plus, new ones they are probably profiting from.
Remember Myspace where everyone's first friend was Tom?

Payback

If someone does me wrong don't worry,
God is on my side, you, betta hide hurry,
The next time you have a curry,
Get prepared to be on the toilet all night,
No, we aint even on a flight,

Mess with me and you'll get it back ten-fold,
Don't worry you can hold on your mug,
It's a tug of war I'm winning without even trying,
You'll soon be crying,
Then it suddenly will get worse,
It will feel like a curse,
Disguised by a silver lining,
The brightest star will dim like Johnny in the shining,

Don't even think about messing with me,
Oh of course you don't want the gifts,
Of course, you don't want the money,
Well why mention it?
I see them pound/dollar signs in your eyes,
The signs have gradually dimmed down,
Whatever crown you had has now been drowned,

Someone who is pure and innocent,
Before, soon showed their true colours,
It's like all the colour from the roses have gone,
The roses have wilted, shrunken, turn to grey,
Hey it wasn't me who needed the break,
I am sorry I didn't need one what you see is what you get,
It's easy talking to a screen,
No to the meet,
I'll find somewhere else to eat,
It's impossible to be perfect all the time,
If you are attracted by the dime,
Then that means money fixes the problem,
Just like Houston,

I aint going to pretend to be perfect,
You can't please everyone,
Rather please someone,
This doesn't mean by money.

Sticking up for people who can't stick up for themselves,
Is what you call friendship,
No, we aint playing battleship,
You just need to have manners.

Between You & I

I know you have a lot of money,
Why is Peter Rabbit 2 out, out?
Didn't your parents tell you to eat your Brussel sprouts,
So that you can climb the highest of mounts,
Some will get it easy,
Others will have to work very hard for only a small amount,
I guess if you were a tout,
Selling so many tickets on the street for gigs lost count,
While others don't and if they do they will get caught,

Whose fault is that?
The one who did it like one time,
What they got paid wasn't even worth a dime,
HAIM just won a BRIT.
They won it for BEST international group,
Let's have some more ice cream I'll have another scoop,
Real people are troops,
A form of exercise is dancing with a hula hoop,
A song you can't get out of your head is a bop, bop, bop,
Did you just get a crop?
Long on top,

There goes the mop,
Clearing up all your grey hair,
While you look down at the floor,
You couldn't believe how many there were,
Mum gets worried over half an inch of grey,
I had long strands of it,
I guess that's what happens while you are in a pandemic.
This ain't fiction,
Check your diction,
I paid mum back my tuition.

At the Time

Things seemed easier at the time,
I wouldn't trade this time for a dime,
What about places that sell cubic zirconia instead,
I just want to lay in my bed,
But I want to get better at walking on my own I said.

If you co-wrote a song how do they split the royalties,
Is it thirty-percent?
I want to wear shorts not jeans,
No one has the right to be mean,
Just because you were keen,
To see the TV show,

Mum saved my big toe,
I was really worried,
I don't like the clippers,
Some people call windscreen wipers,
Flippers as they go left then right,
No matter the car's windscreen height.

I don't want clothing to be tight,
However, I don't want it to be baggy,
Someone got an opinion from their nanny,
His name was Danny,
His girlfriend was called Mandy.

That Feeling

You fall asleep at eight in the evening,
Wait what is the meaning,
To that oh crap where is my cap,
I sometimes need to turn the tap(on),
To help me go a wee,
No, I don't drink tea,
However, I may talk about spilling it,
As that means to gossip about celebrities,
Oh, I hope mum has my keys.

Yes, I do like cheese,
Mature cheddar or blue cheese please,
Don't be a tease,
Did she burn herself or self-harm?
I agree with niall horan no judgement,
How to get out of this predicament.

It's only been a couple of weeks,
She can feel her cheeks with food,
No, she doesn't have to wear a hood,
To be understood,
She is rich but that feeling doesn't make you happy,
Does she have a chap who is her boyfriend?
I don't want to look at the end of book,
That first time I met her she had no mark that had me shook.

TikTok Famous

I created my first batch of merch,
Most of the trees are birch,
No one should self-harm it hurts,
Some people have a rebirth.

I never said I was Damien Hurst,
In fact, I would probably be the worse,
At art without being taught,
Which is what I thought,
Hey hold on art comes in many forms,
Some are there to help more people to mourn,
You can't have a rose without a thorn,
When you lose a loved one beware the man with horns.

Over thirty-thousand followers and you are TikTok famous,
No, it's nothing to be shameless about,
Be proud of yourself,
Don't be like a book and get stuck on the shelf,
They say eighty percent of success is showing up,
If you don't then you won't experience the good times,
I promise there will be more good than bad just like a church bell chimes every
hour.

Have a shower then devour what you have earned,
Go up to the buffet it's your turn,
Tell your mum what you have to learn,
Just like cookie dough it will churn,
Before becoming cookies and crème,
Remember to chase those dreams,
Just like you would watch Netflix and stream,
You don't want to end up as a meme,
Watch out for that laser beam.

You are a part of a team,
Imagine you are someone's strand of hair,
That's there if it wasn't for you it wouldn't be there,
Don't be like the bear in the revenant who gets turned into a coat,
When you are drinking a tipple of alcohol,
Why do about ninety-percent of celebrities have no moles.

Just need to put some lumps of coal on to the fire,
If I continue like this my income might increase,
I know why footballers retire (so early),
Does your sport car need a new tyre (is it flat)?
That's okay there is one in the boot (I spotted a cat).

I do deserve confetti,
Just like Getty,
I have proved and will continue to prove people wrong,

Listening to music is my muse,
So, keep loading and playing them tunes,
Right into my bedroom,
You hear a motorbike outside going vroom vroom.

Christmas BeliEVE

I know that the limits are there to protect me,
When I want my dopamine or oxytocin fix I don't care what the limit be,
Is it too early to spill the tea?
I don't even like tea but I know it's not even about the drink,
It's the name used for new gossip,
Loose lips sink ships.

You be kind 'cos it's the season of giving,
It's what they call being human and living,
They call 'do you want me to drive',
I've already gone to the deep end to go and dive,
Are you going to do a live?
Why so you can troll me?
I will do what I want and be who I want to be!

Christmas time, it's here to have hope,
Did they get me a present? Nope,
I have all these talents,
No, I do not have a chemical imbalance,
The money goes like water,
However, I care about my time,
A lot more than I do, a dime.

Eve was the first woman on earth,
However, Eve wasn't alone,
Adam was there too to set the tone,
If the first two people were Adam and Eve,
Who gave birth to Eve,
Eve was created from Adam's rib,
Is everyone in the world too naïve?

Who the fuck came up with the surname doe,
Oh, let's call them john doe,
He used to be someone's bro,
No one ever found them,
Jane doe just received a gift,
It was time to go in the lift,
She still hasn't
Got John a present,
Jane was told she had one,
She is still using last years,
I could break down in tears.

Why I am spending money on her,
When I don't even have any gift like muhrr,
I said at least I ain't got a bad conscience.

No one gets me a present,
However, there's nothing to show.

Maybe they are already writing my eulogy,
'Cos I am well at it and they are not good at technology.
I don't mean what I learnt,
People's heads will turn,
People who do social networks,
I can't blame them though good luck to the girl,
Who turned her TESCO job into a musical!

Christmas Day

I don't know about you,
However, does Christmas Day,
Fall short when it finally comes around,
It's like we have already eaten loads of mince pies,
Some Christmas cake which is fruit cake with icing on,
That lasts for so long it could be eaten all year after,
What is different is the TV that brings laughter?

For any eighties, nighties or even noughties babies,
They will remember top of the pops as a regular feature,
To tell you the top ten singles and albums,
Plus, random performances from artists,
That are in the top forty that were latest,

Well now top of the pops is only on Christmas day,
And New Year's Eve so only twice a year,
However, don't worry about it the official chart is still on every Friday,
That lasts an hour and forty-five minutes instead of the three hours,
Remember these songs are not ours all though it may seem that way,
It's like a library you rent a book out,
However, you have to return it,

With music you don't have to return it if you buy it you get to keep a copy of it,
Like people living in halls of residence you can call it yours,
It's like you can pay to go on sight-seeing trip with a guide,
However, the trip you take only last for a certain amount of time,
The time is yours,
The money is theirs,
The city that is the sight-seeing place in question,
Gets a mention,
To resolve this tension,

Although, loads of people may visit the same place,
People will download the same song,
However, the song will never be out of stock
As it was never in stock to start with,
For it to be in stock means there's a possibility of it running out,
It won't run out,
Just like the place won't simply vanish,
After the sight-seeing tour is over.

Boxing Day

The main event is over,
However, to make some more money,
Let's reduce the price of all your presents by half,
Don't that make you frustrated you have to take a bath,
To cheer yourself up and relax,
You know what you will be wearing? your tracks,
When I say tracks I don't mean songs I mean tracksuits,
That I got for Christmas,
What was glistening and glittering,
Now was worn and not new anymore,
That was good though they will last for years,
These temporary tears,
Will be forgotten and all will be left are the presents,
They will be worn and used,
Not forgotten about or abused,

Choose, use, or lose,
You can choose to wear any clothes that are presents,
You can use your time to read any books you received,
If you don't choose the presents to wear,
Or use the presents you bought,
You are not worthy of them so you lose them,

Look at your bank balance,
It's not evergreen,
Money doesn't grow on trees,
So please whatever you do freeze for a moment,
Where did you last have that lead,
To charge up your earbuds,
Don't get stuck in the mud,
It can only be downstairs,
Which in cockney is apples and pears,
There's not always going to be someone there,
That you just borrow the cable,
We aren't talking about satellite,
Remember with all might,
Otherwise you aren't going to be able to get to sleep tonight,
Stop the press I found it,
Well mum did,
Thanks mum what would I do without 'ya,

Your brain is known as the grey area, It's what can make you fill an arena like Wembley,
Instead of being backstage being a nobody,
All of the regular Christmas songs are playing in that restaurant,
Which you feel like have been playing over and over,
Don't forget none of them are covers,
There are also new songs that will become regulars.

Christmas Tidings

All of your favourite things about Christmas,
Are allowed from Christmas to the day before New Year's Eve,
Then it's all about a waiting game,
You're a beast that needs to be tamed,
They say you can't listen to Christmas music in October,
Before you know it, Christmas is here,
You're sick of the Christmas songs,
Rather be sick of them then only play them for a couple of days,
Over the Christmas period,

Do you agree?
Or do we agree to disagree!
You don't need to do anything you don't want to,
Do what you want to do,
Spend it however you want just remember,
It's better to be festive than negative,
Be active it's attractive.

Christmas aint just about Christmas dinner,
Well it's a main part of the day,
However, if you don't have the money,
Don't worry all that matters are things that are free which is your family,
Family is sweet as honey, honey never goes off.
Don't bother comparing yourself to others,
There are always going to be people in better situations,
However, there are always going to be in worse,
So, forget that nonsense about you being cursed,

That's an old wives' tale,
What does everyone have in common on Christmas Day,
It's not the TV, it's not the Christmas Dinner,
It's not the money in your back pocket,
It's the festive cheer and love shared to each other,
Which spreads over the smallest to the biggest family.

Sleep My Darling

Apparently three-am to four-am is the witching hour,
It makes all the other hours taste a bit sour,
I feel like a prince in an ivory tower,
Being able to stay up when I want,
My sister calls me a * * *t,
However, she said if you don't make any noise,
Then you can stay up.

Fill up my cup,
Why do I want to stay up?
Because the last two years have been building up to the Japan Olympics,
So, if I make my body used to staying up,
It won't be so hard,
All of my dinner was charred.

I asked a sales assistant in a sports store,
Where did u get your silver chain from,
He said I got it for my birthday,
Do you ever take it off?
He said no I never,
He knows what he is doing,
It is silver sterling silver.

I am listening to Justin Biebers' album it has no filler,
Every tune has a killer beat,
Not one is a dud,
Each tune is like a bud,
Ready to bloom,
That fills the whole room.

Do you ever have every intention to do something?
However, you change your mind and do nothing for the thing you wanted to do,
I do this and I don't know why I do it.

Fancy getting a letter from Google,
Getting me all excited but knowing it was not a cheque,
As I'm nowhere near to reaching the requirements of the YPP,
It said spend one-hundred-and-twenty-pound and get it back,

Where's the logic in that,
What happened to the free seventy-five pound,

Money don't grow on trees,
Growing your YouTube account,
Ain't easy to do why tease me Google!
You know I'm frugal.

You

You will only reach the requirements,
If you end up in the newspaper or on TV,
Multiple times,
How can you have nearly had thirty-one followers,
On one social media network,
Barely have five thousand followers on the other one,
Or even less,
Not even two-hundred-subscribers.

Instagram are now saying 'you can hide likes',
People only post on there in order to get 'likes',
I'm like go take a hike,
No, I'm not wearing Nike,
Or going up the road on my bike.

It's time to take the mic,
Because something ain't right,
I would go asleep but I don't even feel tired,
I'm just fantasizing lord sugar say my business partner,
Now don't get me wrong I know it's harder than anything else,
Will it be on this year,
Or has it disappeared again for another year,
If it has I shed a tear.

Money or Health?

If you live in America,
You have to pay money,
To get better honey,
You will need more than just well wishes,
Just like when a snake hisses.

My Health is priceless,
Throw the dice,
You might win something nice,
Why is it called craps?
Never understood that,
I love how someone who doesn't look like a rapper,
Is one and a good one,
That is my sermon done.

Health is not priceless in USA,
You got told you had to pay how much? aye,
That has just made my day ten times worse,
That I'm afraid will have come out of my purse.

Have you lost it,
Then you're going to need to dig deep in your wallet.
Oh, thankfully I had a good rummage around and I've got it.

As long as you had fun,
You can't force people to enjoy your company,
If they like you they will support you,
However, why is it like a pack of wolves too,
Watch the whole video to the end,
Have they got that time to spend?

I don't understand why create they introduce this three-minute video feature,
Oh three-minute videos but you can just fast forward it,
The content creator must think s***,
Now it is like well I got an hour and four minutes total watch time,
For a three-minute video I got one-hundred-and-ninety-two views.

TikTok is a contradiction,
We are looking to help you promote your posts,
Somehow you can't buy followers or accounts,

However, you can promote your posts,
For like the price of a carousel,
Something isn't right,
What can I smell from TikTok,
Complete bulls**t.

Christmas Alone

There is something worse than a bad Christmas dinner,
Or presents you don't like,
What is it I hear you ask,
While they are thinking,
They are drinking,
Being alone at Christmas time,
All of the lights are lit up,
Christmas lights,
That one house that outdoes every other house in the street.

No amount of lights,
Replaces family,
If you don't have children or cousins visiting you,
You are going to feel blue,
Not from the winter chill,
From the red heart that turns to grey,
No one to say hey,
No one to say we can make one extra seat at the table,
For you so you are not alone,
Who is ruling and who is on the throne,

The queen will have to face Christmas alone for the first time,
If no one visits her this year on Christmas Day,
She is very wealthy as in money,
However, not as in honey,
She has to put her game face on,
Pull herself together to do a Christmas speech,
Some people are just leeches,
You get them what they want,
However, they would come back for your eyeballs,
If you let them,
There has to be line to not cross,
Jesus was crucified for our sins,

Just so we could live,
No one is perfect,
You wouldn't be human,
If you woro,
Even people like Beyoncé or Michael Bublé,
Even they have their flaws,
Heck, Beyoncé has already recorded a song having flaws and all,

So, stand tall and stand proud,
Don't compare yourself to anyone else,
As there is not another you out there,
Just think while you feel lonely,
If you believe in God you are holy,
Jesus will direct you to other people who are also holy too.

Some people feel lonely in a crowd,
No matter how loud,
The music is playing,
Or the atmosphere is busy,
You are not the only one,
Feeling this way,
So, dance like nobody is watching,
Stop checking your watch for the time,
Each five minutes,
There's nowhere you need to be,
Other than here.

Christmas Morning

Look how it changes from when you were an excited child,
To a sensible adolescent,
On to a grown-up adult,

When you are an excited child,
You go to sleep early on Christmas eve,
Only to wake up at 2 in the morning,
Jumping on their parents' bed,
'Quick, it's time to open my presents',
'I have been waiting the whole month for this day',
The excited child says,
The sensible adolescent,
Is more grown up but not completely,
'It's six in the morning time to open my presents under the tree',
These feelings are priceless over their presents,
We are having turkey not pheasant,

The grown-up adult is like 'It's ten-am time to open my presents',
Okay, okay at least it is a respectable hour,
For once, the parents say,
The adult drove round to their parent's house,
Especially for this.

They have their wife and one kid of their own,
Back at their house,
'I know what it feels like now being woke up at two-am in the morning now',
'You think back on them days and can't believe that used to be me',
'Hahaha, how does it feels being the parent and not the child?' His dad asked,
'It had me reaching for the hip flask laughing out loud' The grown-up adult
replied.

'I just popped round to share some memories with you,'
'Thank you, son, we appreciate it',
'OMG you got me a PS5' the grown-up adult said.

'Never too old to play games!' The dad said to his son.
'I'll hold you to that!' The son said to his dad.

'Sure, once it's all set up, invite me round!' The dad said.
'Cool, I definitely will do!' The son replied.

'We have a bigger house if you want to pop round to ours for Christmas dinner!' The son invited his parents!

'Yes, we were able to get a turkey!' The son added.

'Love or hate them, we are doing Brussels!' The son said.
'I love the Brussels' The mum answered.

Christmas Lunch

We always have lunch right before Top of The Pops,
It's a Christmas tradition that I need to go a wee,
Throughout Top of the pops on Christmas Day,
However, they won't remember 'cos I always hold it in,
While I heard mum scrapping the crumbs in the bin,

Mum don't mind listening to the weekly chart on a Friday,
Well that is what Top of The Pops is on Christmas Day,
After TOTP, we always watch the Queen's speech,
If my memory serves me right,
Martin Lewis always say watch out for
That 1 litre of Baileys for just 9GBP,
Good luck trying to get that this year,
Christmas cheer may have to replace it with tears,
Of joy; No, I ain't no Chris hoy or Claire foy,

What's going to be TV this Christmas,
Well I don't know but don't rule out A Muppet's Christmas Carol,
Or Frozen 2; Or the live action version of The Jungle Book,
Or maybe the live action version of Beauty and the Beast.

Everyone knows Christmas is really for the kids,
As you can remember when you were a kid at Christmas,
Like Home Alone, 'keep the change ya filthy animal',
Every child who is now a grown adult remembers that quote,
Don't choke on your Brussel sprouts,
Your parents are like what? When you shout it out!

You had a cashmere Burberry scarf; from years and years ago,
One of the most expensive things I ever was to own,
That was it! All my Christmas allowance blown,
Oh well, at least I didn't drown,
So, there's no reason to frown,
You just felt down.

Mum says 'it's okay I don't need anything this Christmas',
However, when you get her a present you see her eyes grow three times
The size, her heart starts to beat, beat faster,
If that's what happens when someone who doesn't want anything gets
something,
What must happen to someone that actually does want something;

I worry 'cos they will probably fall head over heels;
With all of the Christmas feels.

Good Let's Go!

The greatest opportunity at the moment isn't TikTok,
It is Clapper,
I don't mind using Clapper it's harder grow on there,
However, when you go live,
You get gifts like Clive,
You can chat; have a deep dive,
In your videos,
Obviously, I enjoy it as I am aejmedia,
I get to do what I want because I'm disabled,
I may not be able to walk without a Zimmer frame,
But sitting on this sofa or at the table,
When it comes to success,
They say that achievement is mine,
No, it isn't time to start buying pine (trees).

People come up with their own catchphrases,
Creating a brand is the key to your successes,
Messes are what you make when you are figuring your road to a mix of fun
and income,
Why are baked beans in a tin?
I don't know maybe that's why I am thin,
When I'm deep in thought I tend to scratch my chin!

I have gone five weeks with just my phone,
Just to set the tone,
I can have a few ice cream scoops in an ice cream cone.
So, don't talk to me about possessions,
I have gone without them when needed,
I even went without reeses pieces.

I ain't being cheeky,
If I tell a joke I will go hehe,
In my summer I will stay in a tepee.
No, I wouldn't just testing you that aint me.

Stuck

Stuck in the deep end,
Need a friend,
Off byheart I can only think of two,
What if I drown in the pool,
He was such a cool dude,
The pool was a clean deep light blue.

Would anyone notice if I slipped away,
Stuck in the pool, body lifeless for most of the day.
Quick someone help there's someone in the pool,
They are in the deep end and they are quite short,
Oh no hope he hasn't died in there,
Just like when I got run over,
Mum isn't there she is nowhere to cover
Herself with an excuse.

I have to realise I have to rely on the kindness of strangers,
I ain't even talking about doppelgangers,
Anyway, mum can go away from me,
She will, I'm just having a tea (she says),
Wait I need to go for a wee (she does).

Stuck in the packed crowd now lockdown has eased,
I can't be paid my pay check, so this one is not pleased,
I got teased the other day when I saw it was ten years,
Since Amy Winehouse died I couldn't fight back the tears.

I poured my heart out on TikTok then I realised they don't care,
When I poured my heart out it was like a glass of blood go from full to empty
like I was a hare,
I sat on the chair the fabric was beige,
Now it is a deep maroon from the blood,
I guess I didn't realise how much bad luck I had.

Luck

I never see some of my friends in grow lives,
Yet they are like wow two-hundred-thousand followers,
How though I have been on the app for nearly two years,
I only see them in their own lives,
Yes, I love cheese and chives (crisps),
How much is it luck and how much is hard work?
There a higher probability of seeing the queen twerk,
Like nought-percent so get back to work.

Luck or Karma?
Luck you have no control over,
However, Karma you don't,
However, if you focus on the result
Here is where superstition comes in,
It does what it says on the tin.

You need to be authentic,
Expect nothing in advance,
Just like when you take a stance,
What do you believe?
Also, could it be fate,
Where your life is a game to be played with some hate,
As long as I can have some steak.

Christmas Tags

Whenever it's Christmas and before you open your presents,
Does your mum leave the price tags on them?
Is this to say look I want you to behave,
Be good, let's all have a great time this Christmas,
Who knows what's going to happen,
In the next twelve months,
Don't get angry, don't go to sleep on an unresolved argument,
There's enough anger on the TV,
We don't need it in this house too,
Let's not make each other feel blue,

Blue Christmas is only a song,
Not real life, not at the moment,
Time is precious, just like Gollum says about the gold ring,
In lord of the rings,

Make sure you leave everything as it was,
Ready for the rest of the festive season,
Christmas is not just one day,
There is the month of advent in December,
In the run up to Christmas,
You can't have Christmas Eve without Christmas Day,
As Owl City sings,
As the elves put the finishing touches onto your presents,
Don't let anyone tell you that you are a peasant,
It's not true and it's not pleasant,
You are present and you deserve all of the presents you receive.

Maybe mum leaves the tags to say look that's a lot of money,
You should be very grateful I didn't need to be that generous,
You'll be like I know and I don't take anything for granted,
Forever stay enchanted,
With the innocence of the feels that this festive season,
Brings this Christmas.

Christmas Riddle

Mum was like what?
'Keep up with what's hot' I said,
Leave it in the bowl,
Don't be a troll,
Especially not at Christmas,
That would be blasphemous,

Confuse them,
You're going to need them,
Don't explain it to them,
Let them figure it out,
No need to shout,
About what you don't understand.

I get it you are a fan,
Don't forget to top up your tan,
Everyone is Santa Claus' Stan,
You say you don't know what a Stan is,
It means they are your number one fan,

What's the difference between a fan and a Stan?
A fan will only be there when you are riding high,
A Stan will be there when you are riding high or flying low,
A fan won't be there for the bad times whereas a Stan will be,
It is like an unwritten rule that every Stan follows,
No matter whether you are short or tall, big or small,

A Stan will be there to pull you up,
A Stan will be there so you don't fall in the first place,
No matter what.

Boxing Day
Morning

It's true what they say,
You don't know what you got till it's gone,
They were not irreplaceable,
However, it's like smoking one last cigarette,
Once it's gone, there's no more of that make,
You can't take it if it ain't there,
I will never meet them again,
I still have their number in my phone,
I still felt like that was the end,
No more communication just anecdotes,
Like writing this poem,
Staying up to 3am,

'Cos the creativity only comes around in the middle of night,
If it's a new moon tonight,
The alpha pack of wolves are awake and roaming in the forest,
While you stay awake and stay alert,
I have a search for my teddy bear called Bert,
To you he is Bert,
To me he is Bertie,

Are you getting thirsty,
I am over thirty,
I bought a little book of sleep,
To help me get back to sleep,

However, I choose to stay up,
I can't write creatively when the sun rises,
No matter what my goal or what the price is,
No one is superior over anyone,
There are only human beings in the right place,
At the right time,

It's not what you know,
It's who you know,
Is there such thing as a million-dollar-couch?
I love my hoodies as they have a pouch,
I have a caring touch that heals most things,

I have a big heart that defeats hate and gives you a tough skin,
Chuck away every song you wrote but now hate,
As Jesus died for our sins,
So just take it on the chin,
Fin.

Free Speech

Last time I checked this app was for free speech,
Not bullying, it was two against one in the pk,
Don't worry they won't see this as they won't buy it,
If they do buy it oh I thought you was broke,
You know that bloke everyone missed,
However now was this just a play on our emotions,
They are called coins but for reference let's call them tokens,
People go on there because they are broken,

Anyone remember that song?
You going to reap just what you sow,
You do something bad, something bad will happen to you,
You do something good,
Keep going it's what you should,
Do but don't be fake,
Like sideshow bob you will be stepping on rakes,
How much can you take,

It's like people's opinions,
Simon Cowell tells the truth,
The feedback isn't all smooth,
There will be some boos,
These are your Karen's and Felicia's,
Believe it or not,
What are the male versions?
The Fred's and teds,
Have they taken their meds?
What do you think?
They reached the brink,
The bad thoughts were so loud,
Even those they were never said,
By Fred, they are on the mend,

Will you be their friend?
Still well if you are reading this,
That means you bought it,
So, put your fist in the air,
Declare you were here,
If I make it big,
Yes, and I love a fig,
Not a fan of a twig,
However, some people look good in a wig.

Talent

My money isn't dripping off of me,
Surely if I'm talented I shouldn't be giving things away for free,
No, I don't want a cup of tea,
I'll have a cup of joe,
Don't treat me wrong,
There are many others to replace you,
Just think about a cashier in a supermarket,
All they do is scan the items form the convey belt,
Then push them to turn the end of the scanning station,
This doesn't require any qualification,

How come people with few or no Qualification,
Have thousands or even millions of followers,
What am I doing wrong?
Yes, I know in Australia flip flops are called thongs,
You can't eat your meal without a fork with three prongs,

Should I create a book or sell each poem or song,
Separately as Ne-Yo did with irreplaceable to Beyoncé,
Let's face it some songs are just better sang by some fiancé,

I wasn't on the app for ten days,
I got no clap backs asking where I had gone,
Kyle got ten clap backs including mine,
Everyone else thought where,
Shedding a tear,
It aint the first lot of tears they shed either,
I so want to gamble but I can't I need a breather,

Some female country singer can't say that they paved the way,
For her to become the country superstar in present day,
As she takes the mick of her in a very popular song,
It is one of their well-known ones which is wrong.

Insomnia

Something needs to be wrong with you,
You need to have something clouding your view,
You need to either have an inspirational backstory,
Do something that's never been done before,

By the way the people that cross me,
WILL NOT be acknowledged,
You showed your true colours,
GO and pray 'cos that's the only way,
You will make it through the day,

If I come into money,
None of its yours honey,
No need to worry,
As you said you were not doing it for the money,
Well then let's test that,
Let's see how much of a brat,
You turn into,
If you don't know the less it will hurt,
You have an uncontrollable thirst,

The only way you will get my money,
Is it if I created a will and left something to you,
My family will get some because they don't turn on by the flick of a switch,
No, they aren't bitches,
Pitches of sangria in Portugal we used to have,
Now I can't have any alcohol all I have to do is save,

My mental health is under control,
I had a better time on the original app,
The one without the clap,
The one where you can't show your baps,
However, you can wear caps.

It's no secret that I'm a night owl,
If you don't know that by now,
Are you even my friend?
Are you just jumping on trend?
When will this end?
Will you break or bend?

I guess we will have to live our lives,

Let's see who thrives,
Will it be them or will it be me?
That will be decided over a cup of tea
Of course, a PK AS WELL,
Don't dwell,
It could be worse.

Autumn Angels

The last two Novembers,
I have been able to my grow my social media accounts,
Without limits is this just the magic of the end of autumn,
As when December comes it's not only the start of a new month,
It's the start of a new season; winter is coming soon and the start
Of advent, those who believe in it I will get an advent calendar,
However, not before I go to the dentist as my teeth are hurting,
I got to stop eating chocolate,
Or food with high sugar content,

I want to have a gingerbread latte,
However, I feel it maybe too sweet on my teeth,
My teeth always seem to hurt around this time of the year,
Maybe it's because of mince pies and Christmas cake,
I feel like that person in the story of Matilda who had wanted some chocolate
cake,
They had to eat the whole thing,
No, I won't have any cake thanks,

Thank you to the angels watching over me,
You don't know how grateful I am that you are here and you are near,
Making all of my fear go away,
On this new day,
We are half way through the week,
Isn't it going quick,
I got less than a week to meet my goal,
I want to get to 10k followers by December,
The start of advent,
I might have to part with some cents,
I will have to have common sense,

If I want to stay up to midnight,
I can't be staying up to three,
Even though I need to decide what's more important,
Publishing another book,
Or growing my social media.

I ain't superman,
If I want to achieve success,
I have to decide and manifest what I want,

It's easier to grow my social media,

Than it is writing poems,
As I can only write them in the middle of the night,
They ain't even dirty they're just unique.
I only had three hours of sleep last night,
You only live once,
What is more important to you?
Success or Sanity,
Well sanity obviously,
Then success,
These Christmas poems are only appropriate,
During this festive season,
No other reason.

I feel I could really succeed at this,
If I continue to give it my all,
If I have a fall,
I get back up,
I stand tall.
The trees shed their leaves,
That ain't going to happen to me,
The harder I try, the more likely I will succeed,
Just breathe in the hate, then breath it out leaving only love.
Love myself, love the air,
Love the world, love each word I speak,
Go from love to an affinity, love my body,
Block out all of the hate,
Leaving only fate.

Christmas

Surprise

I thought I'll have a quick gander,
There probably isn't much to see,
They probably don't have a big sale,
I don't have money like Gareth bale,
This is just a festive tale,
While we are in the pandemic still,
Oh, here comes the bill,
20% off the grand total that goes straight in the till,
If you want to give the sale assistant a tip,
Make sure it goes in their zip[pocket],
So, they can dine on that or helps in some way,
It's the little things that brighten someone's day,

As burger king say 'HAVE IT YOUR WAY',
It's sunny today like it's a day in late May,
Hey, look as long as I receive the money back for the DVDs,
I buy them even though I don't like selling them,
I easy made the money back,
For the shopping today,
Money, money, money,
The winner takes it all,
You rise and they fall,

I don't need any minimum wage job,
I'm making money from other means,
Okay, so I never got a Saturday job when I was a teen,
Look what has happened to the shop I gave my CV too,
They have shut down,
I ain't going to frown,
I still hate clowns,
I'm taking over your town,
With this recognition I have got,
Okay, I take the money pound by pound,
Until I become as rich as those that wear crowns,
Do I have a gated community?

No but I'm working on it,
Hey, if the shoe fits then wear it,
I was told I had a zit,
I had no time for it,
Just focused on looking great,
Alright mate,
Is this fate?
A sweet one at that,
Don't forget your hat,
Don't go in there for ten minutes,
I just did a number two,
Do you know what a number three is?
If you don't it's when you go both a number one and two,
At the same time,
I ain't talking about the herb,
I need to write the blurb,
Some people are big on YouTube,
As they were told to not be seen or heard,
Out of sight, out of mind,

Don't let them put the cotton wool over your eyes,
You don't have to dress formal dress casual but cool.
Who is in control the vidIQ of the watch-time hours?
There's something really wrong with at the moment,
It was 131 watch time hours now it's 129,
It's like you're on a bus that goes forwards two stops,
then back two,
I have emotions, I have feelings and I am affected,
All of my content is my own,
I have never collaborated with anyone,
So, it's starts with a blank page,

The content just comes to me while listening to music,
Who is it I listen to? Well that would be telling wouldn't it,
Instead of pen and paper; how about just a blank document,
No need for argument, even if I fart,
Each blank page is a new start,
For a new poem,
So, go and tell them,
Have a blessed day,
Okay like Selena Gomez
sings kill 'em with kindness,
Try practicing mindfulness.

Now or Never

Jessie J is right,
It's now or never,
In order to have a good Christmas,
Or xmas the love is there,
X marks the spot,
Sometimes the C gets replaced by a X,

If I don't publish these Christmas Poems,
This year I will have to wait a whole year,
Before the festive season comes around again,
Who knows where or what will happen to me a year from now,
No one knows,
So just focus on the now and not the never,

Never means it'll never be published but it will be,
Trust me, manifest it and it will come,
Just like a set of drums, drums, drums,
Hum, hum, hum,
Sexy from your head to your bum,
I can't forget your pins or legs some say,
Just stay and put your legs over me,
Which I don't mind at all wanna a pk?
Okay they say with enthusiasm,

Like Gollum says my precious to the gold ring,
One ring to rule them all,
Stand up and stand tall,
It's nearly the end of fall,
Take your shoes in the hall[way],
After coming in from the mall.

There are two of you,
There's only one of me,
Not to drink it but to spill the tea,
What's the latest spillage then,
Have you just come back from Dragons Den?
Or are they currently filming it for next year?
I let out a tear,
'Cos the youngest ever dragon is now twenty-nine,
Six years younger than the twenty-nine-year-old,
Will he invest in anything?
Also, is he replacing anyone 'cos I love Sara Davis,

I know she is doing strictly come dancing,
Is that to promote her career or is it her swan song,
Am I right or am I wrong?
They pick up the panini with hot prongs,
I always say cut it in half please,
I don't care what people say
You can't say no to a ham and mozzarella panini,
Not even the queenie,
Don't be a meanie,
Put back on your beanie.

Father Future

How many years do I have left?
I ask while looking at some of the books still on my bookshelf,
Some of these books are nearly as old as me,
I guess it will just happen suddenly,
They say my disability doesn't reduce my life expectancy,
That may be true as whatever will be will be.

I fell asleep and had a dream,
I felt like I was on holiday which was cool,
Come be part of the stream.

Where Father's Day is just another day,
No need to pray as I think my dad has turned into a vengeful spirit,
Tell the DJ to hit it,
I don't want this s***,
I never did anything to dad,
Nothing that was bad.

Why is it the 4G doesn't work in the house,
I keep as quiet as a mouse,
My sister doesn't know I'm awake,
Here we go another goal scored by Harry Kane,
The lion is so beautiful that our mascot is three lions on a shirt,
No one got hurt,
Pass me a yoghurt,
Peaches and cream,
You scream with joy,
You just won twenty pounds and you're not even Chris Hoy.

Adoption may be on the cards,
If I live a long life,
I need someone to look after me,
Whether that's a he or a she,
Someone who doesn't charge a fee,
Then I would be happy.
.
Father Future,
If you are going to be a spirit,
You gotta know when to hit it,
I mean when it is time for me sit back,

You have to treat mum like you're not lacking,
Sister make sure you are not slacking.

Healthy in Moderation

I will probably will be single lucky I had a relationship,
It was lust, luck, love, light and we did everything there was to do,
It may not have been long,
We did doggy, missionary and other positions,
From the karma sutra in addition,
Is it in addition or addiction?
We did it three times in one day,
Well our sexual organs are for what exactly they it says they are,

Sex!
Yes, Please as Austin Powers would say,
Let's have a lazy day but remember to stay(awake),
For the syndicate,
I thought never entered a syndicate before,
I have been watching every week,
This time is different,
I have entered,
I know I'm self-centred.

I have already made the money back,
I won twenty-pound on an instant win game,
I paid twenty-four-pound for an entry,
So, I just need to win four-pound more,
I know I will win more than that though,
Forget the cookie dough, I'm going win some actual dough.

If I didn't look after me,
Who would just like the bushes and trees,
They look after themselves,
Before anyone else,
You need to look after your health,
Which helps you look after your self-worth.

Self-belief is the most important thing,
It controls everything,
From the way you talk to the way you sing,
What can I hear that ka-ching ka-ching?

Tills are open,
You have won,
A wad of cash,
It's time to dash.

Love Is Regained

I hadn't had a cuddle from mum,
Since before the pandemic,
I had one yesterday and I felt so much love,
Just as if I was a dove.

So much love,
Love,
Love,

I know why there were no pheromones,
This is because my sister and my mum keep swapping perfumes,
I'm like that's my sisters' smell,
I don't want mum to smell like my sister,
My sister does love me,
Not as much as my mum though,

Also, when mum wears my sisters' clothes,
It's a brain f* *k,
That is not what I want,
Let's go on a hunt,
For the love that is blunt.

My sister's eyes turn into pound signs,
She is thinking I better start to be nice,
What if he becomes mega-rich,
Richer than she could ever imagine,
I wouldn't even need the genie's three wishes,
Yes, I do hoard things but that's none of your business,
I wouldn't need to hit the bullseyes on each archery board,
I know that for sure.

Shop Until Drop

When it hits the stroke of midnight,
On black Friday you know where I'll be,
Online try to get bargains galore,
You don't need to wear yourself out,
Every shop is at your fingertips,
I aint talking sharpies,
I'm talking exclusive amazon prime early deals,
Which gives you all of the feels,

You feel welcome, you feel wanted,
So, don't take it for granted,
Just like how each song that charted (on top 40),
What was that you farted?
LMAO well a lot of people say,
If you feel comfortable around them when they stay,
You will fart and the other person doesn't mind,
We are all human you can't spell human without man,

I never burped for twenty-five years,
Sometimes you can have tears of joy,
As well as tears of sadness,
What do you call an important woman?
A Madame, a dame, a duchess or a governess,
They all have the same thing in common,
They worked hard all their life to get given that title.

Game show hosts always ask what would spend the money on if you won?
I'm like what do they do when they score a hole in one?
You don't get to see that!
I hate to sound like a brat,
I would probably buy some more hats,
I would have more chats,
I aint going to reward anyone that have been horrible to me,
Let's just wait and see,
Do the trolls become bees,
Keep flying around you like you are honey,
Are they expecting money?
No way, out of sight, out of mind.

We could have really been something,
We could have been great friends,
However, you were throwing insults at me,

Like we were playing volleyball so bad I couldn't see,
For a while there.

When I said drop I didn't mean from bullying,
I meant from shopping,
That was what was popping,
I aint talking popping candy,
I love Mandy,
Aint that dandy,
I would have myself a shandy,
That would be handy.

Friend or Foe?

I didn't tell her,
However, I told him,
Sunny Jim,
So, she has the vehicle that run me over at sixteen,
Stop! I need my spleen.

Okay not the exact one,
It feels and looks like it weighs a tonne,
I should know I got hit by one,
Hun!

Is she putting on a front,
Twice in a month,
There is something wrong,
I gotta be strong,
I feel like I connect with her,
But every time I think this,
She proves that I didn't at all,
Not even at the mall.

She acts friendly,
However, is she?
I get to eat out before coming home,
The actual day I've no problem with,
If I arrange it at the last minute,
I ain't gonna win it,
I get the bull****,
I was with him for nearly four years,
And there were no tears.

Sure, at Christmas time,
I might miss one week or two,
However, this is the start of the summer.
What a summer bummer.

Friend or Foe,
The show must still go on,
I hope this past month gono,
Is not a sign of things to come?

If she is a foe,

She is just like an ingrown toenail,
Easy for it to get out of control,
Like getting sunburn and developing a new mole.

She is obviously rich,
Err hello she has one of the most expensive cars on the market,
She knows where to park it,
How to start it,
And stop it,
I think she enjoys the job,
As she started last year,
Everyone gives her a cheer,
She already has enough money to last her the year.

If her nan is anything like mine was,
She's probably the apple in her nan's eye.
I ain't talking about the brand,
Just look the massive ring on her hand,
Watch out to see what she finds bland.

I didn't go out this weekend,
Oh, I just remembered what has just come to an end.
It was her birthday on Saturday.
That explains things, it all fits into place now.
She didn't want to chance having a bad day wow.

It all makes sense.
No reason to be tense,
That explains it all,
No need for Clarissa,
Her boyfriend is there saying here is another piece of birthday cake for ya!

.

Christmas Caper

Superman doesn't need to wear a cape,
To be a superhero,
He just needs to love his kids,
Including his daughter AND son,
Not just his daughter AND leave his son out in the cold,
He should allow his daughter cheese AND his son,
He shouldn't wait UNTIL the cheese turns mouldy,
He should give BOTH of his children cuddles and kisses,
He shouldn't just comfort his daughter and NOT his son,

That's why I yearn for TV shows which have a father-son relationship,
To see how it should be AND HOW I actually have it,
It's okay to kiss AND cuddle your son,
If only you did MORE than just once,
I had to have a mental health condition because I got any comfort,
From my dad; I know I speak for a lot of people when I say this,
As other adults in my generation have either experienced the same thing,
Or no relationship at all,
Mum is having to be the mother and father since my dad passed,
She does a pretty damn good job at it as well.

It makes me think my dad's condom split when they were having me,
Were they EVEN wearing one,
I DON'T know if they were trying for a baby,
Definitely MAYBE I have to say,
I think MANY people would agree,
You DON'T need to have a superpower,
To be a decent superhero,
Just show LOVE when your child or children shows love to you,
He was a man who said very few words,
He would come in watch tv,
While waiting for his dinner,
Which mum would do for him,
Every night except for Sunday,
My dad was known for doing a good Sunday roast,

He was good at that,
However, he gave mum the most food,
Then he would give my sister a lot more vegetables and chicken,
Than me no wonder I was so scrawny,
I was very thin but my sister always got more,

Even if she couldn't eat it all.
I wish it was just Christmas time he did it,
However, this wasn't the case he did it the whole year through,
Until my mum took over doing the Sunday roast,
She was fair; all it takes is for you to have a big enough heart to love your whole family,
Not just your wife and daughter.
Instead having a narrowminded small heart,
He should have had treated me the same respect as my sister,
I could've sworn there was a lump of coal there where his heart was supposed to be,
I never felt loved the same way he loved my sister and mum,
That my dad did, he would never smile and he wasn't comforting,
To me anyway, I can't count for others but from I have heard it seems to be the same story,

If you are a dad reading this PLEASE SHOW your kids some affection and comfort it costs nothing AND it would mean so much that any tablets would,
Why do they call a five-year wedding anniversary – wood,
My interpretation is this wood comes from a tree,
Wood grows into a tree,
Just like your marriage is growing in years,
Forget the beer goggles or the rose-tinted-glasses,
You either love your partner or not,
You either love just your children and not your spouse,
As this does happens to some marriages,
Remember marriages aren't just for Christmas,
They are for life,
As the standard vows say love one another,
Till death do us part.

Father Christmas

Father Christmas has been more of a father to me,
Than my own dad has been,
Yet people say he doesn't exist,
Well why do I feel love for him more than my real dad,
My dad,
my dad,
my dad,

When I was growing up the magic was thinking
and praying Father Christmas exists,
Through the foggy mist,
As a kind of twist,

To think one person would travel around the whole planet,
Coming down the chimney to deliver our presents,
Which was impossible because we don't even have a chimney,
I don't even think I knew what a chimney was at that age anyway,
Or what a sleigh was like,
You know there's something wrong,
When you can recall the ghost face mask as clear as day,
Yet I hadn't seen elves working in the workshop.
Except for fake ones in the film called Elf.

It was better to believe in Santa Claus,
Than my dad who couldn't give a damn about me,
I used to love to decorating the Christmas tree,
Personally, because I saw the joy it gave my mum to decorate it,
All of the Christmas nostalgia, came flooding back,
Which is what the festive season does,
It reminds me of the good times and if you're lucky less bad times than good.

I Dream of Christmas

When I dream of Christmas,
I dream of the nostalgia it brings,
How mum says every year,
Don't get anything for me,
Yet she has moment of glee,

When I tell her I got her a little something?
All mums are like you shouldn't have,
Why shouldn't I?
You are being a mother and a father to both of us,
She is a darling and would do anything for either me or my sister,
What I enjoy most about Christmas,
Is the togetherness,
We all eat our Christmas dinners,
At the dinner table,
At the same time,

Then we watch Christmas TV,
I'm normally always on Facebook,
However not this year,
It will feel different,
However, a lot of it is fake anyway,
Your friends trying to outdo each other,
With their pictures and videos of them;
Pretending how perfect their family life
Is and it's supposedly better than you could ever imagine.

When really, it's lonely and grey,
They don't know how to get through the day,
How something so different;
Can be turned into an imaginary Merry Christmas.

Covid-Free Christmas

Santa, is it too much to ask to have a covid-free Christmas?
Can we all be together like we couldn't be last year?
Whatever happens can we not be alone,
I'm looking forwards to the Christmas decorations going up,
Fill something up in my cup,
Not coffee, Oreo hot chocolate will do,
I'm blowing on the hot chocolate,
As it is hot just like your dad,
Except he has a coffee,

I don't want to take to another covid test,
It does say IF though which means it's voluntary,
I don't have covid and I've heard the flow tests don't work,
So, no I won't taking the covid-19 test,
Why me and not the other the other 60 million people in the country?
If I want to stay up and write Christmas poems I should be able too.

Winter Comes Early

Don't leave me out in the cold,
I said like a plea and I sounded bold,
Do what you are told,
Your parents speak wisdom,
I don't mean Norman,
Hello my dear,
Do you need a cup of festive cheer?

While I'm here there's no reason for your fear,
Sometimes it can be therapeutic letting out a tear,
We are as they say mere mortals,
All human beings needing water, food and oxygen,
To survive, even if you think your favourite celebrities are immortals,

Have you noticed these celebrities have no moles?
You look at them I aint wrong,
Choose a song for us to escape in,
It's does what it says on the tin,
Don't waste food and put it in the bin,
That is a sin,
Other people would have loved that food,
Don't bite your nose to spite your face,
It's full of distaste,
Eat your dinner at your own pace,
Know that it isn't a race,

However, winter is here even though it's still autumn,
It's supposed to snow tonight,
Be careful and don't go out without a need you might,
Need to stay in and entertain each other,
Don't let it get you down and say why bother?
Loads of people love you,
So, you have a great day,
If you may.

If You Know Me

If you know me,
You know I love an alliteration,
To set things into motion,
Apparently the one time I didn't feel sceptical,
The covid-19 vaccine we both had,
Doesn't work I'm so mad.

When I say we I mean me and mum?
So, it can give you blood clots why were we so dumb,
We rushed in and had the AstraZeneca,
Apparently, it is only thirty-three percent effective to the delta variant.

You are not allowed to mix jabs either,
Why do you think I'm spending my money like water?
Didn't GSCE Science teach you anything?
It taught me many things but never a pandemic.
No one expected a pandemic in real life,
Except for the writers of heroes,
I had to switch from frosties to cheerios',
To preserve my enamel against the sugar,
Why do people call their electronics 'her',
Oh, she aint f*****g working again.

Try mindfulness they say,
That is all well and good,
Mindfulness don't keep you warm at night so I've got my cap on and hood,
The fan keeps turning off and on,
Dad's spirit is here tonight,
If I learnt anything from supernatural,
It is that a spirit can survive and transfer from one object to the next.

What do Sam and Dean do to rid the house of bad spirits,
Burn the bones, burn the body, burn the ashes.

If dad got buried he wouldn't be in this house,
He would be six-feet-under in the ground,
Where he would just be a skeleton,
Do you believe in possession?
Like in the harry potter and the deathly hallows movies,
Ron becomes possessed,
Then harry does,

I don't recall Hermione becoming possessed though.

I wonder if many of this generation that are born now,
Are called Hermione,
I never heard that name before the harry potter series!

I love Krispy-Kremes,
I will say this again because it's the truth,
Sometimes less is more,
Like a round doughnut no hole but filled with raspberry.
Or chocolate with custard.

I thought vanilla came from vanilla pods,
They don't, they come from black strips of vanilla filling,
Aint that interesting!

F * * * Off Father's Day

It's just another day,
So why should I go asleep,
Wake up and feel like s***,
I aint gonna pretend my dad was a saint,
Or a sinner I just feel sorry for mum,
It's nearly seven years since my dad died,
I can still picture it clear as day,

Waking up at ten a.m. on a Sunday,
Dad's veins went all purple and blue,

The ambulance took five hours to come,
None of dad's colleagues probably found out.

I think mum was too emotional to tell them,
The real reason was she wanted to ring my dad's work number to hear his voice,
She got her ** *t together and rang them on the Tuesday morning,
Yeah, we were all mourning as well.

Loyal to Who?

Do you keep on top of your loyalty cards?
It's like a got a ticket to mars,
Next thing I know I saw Lewis Hamilton in formula one car,
Me and my friends went into the bar,
My name is charlotte but you can call me char.

I can't have a wallet,
I'm afraid I might lose it,
I don't want mum to say ****,
So, mum my podcast is a hit.

Really people actually like listening to you,
Yeah, I've proved you and my sister wrong,
Ding, dong,
Ding, dong,
Ding, dong,

I finally got my money from clapper,
I was like clapper better have my money,
Otherwise they will need more than manuka honey,
What happened to the bunnies now Hugh Heftner has passed away,
Are they going to get employed at hooters?
Not to be confused with the horn,
Next to the steering wheel,
Now that is a true cheap thrill.

Apparently, James Bond has a license to kill,
It was only meant to be pretend at the cinema,
I think he got his swiss-army-knife literally,
Daniel Craig behaved bitterly,
They didn't even go to Italy,
What's with this summer it's chilly.

Has English and Australia swapped weather,
I think I think still have heather,
Let's pull out the sweater,
Even though it should be t-shirt weather.

I want to watch American's Got Talent,
However, sister was off last week which was apparent,
The last thing we need is another Karen,
Or a Darren who only loves himself,
The clock has just truck twelve,
It is now midnight.

Delivery

You don't have to be Shania Twain,
Or Even Carrie Underwood,
If you have charisma in abundance,
You may join for a dance,
No hesitation this is the chance,
You don't even need to be from France.

If you have a great stance,
Strong, hot and heavy,
You are better than many,
Just chuck a penny in the well,
Let's have a game of monopoly with these girls,

We are all adults here,
With no onlookers,
So, what if she is a hooker,
Most women are one when you take the sleeve off of the hardback,

Have I discovered that in order to be clever you have to have a mental illness?
Stop this conversation it's time to look after the lioness',
Wait! No one is possessed,
Was this all just a test.

Have you stuffed a pair of socks down there?
No why would you ask that,
Because you are packing a lot during this chat,
I think we might need DPD,
In order to give it to her.

Woop Woop

This is what you say when something good happens,
Especially, when you weren't expecting it,
Like winning a PK battle,
Don't forget to count those cattle,
To drift off to sleep without the hassle,
These so-called remedies do not work,
Just like someone who is disabled can't twerk,

Woop Woop, it's a time for a celebration,
Remember actions speak louder than words,
So, go on and play that game of scrabble,
Go and travel with your family it will be fun,
It will be worth it, it will make you happy,
If you are on TikTok, carry on tapping on the screen,
It will bring more people into the live,
There's a higher chance of getting gifts,
That's what the host is really thinking,
Why else would they want hundreds or thousands in their live?
Not to have a chat believe me,

You can't chat with five-hundred viewers,
They say it's a grow party,
However, people who are growing,
Feel bad for not rewarding the host,
If there is over five-hundred in the live,
At least one-hundred people are probably gifting,
That is why they are saying grab the gifters,
Then the host feels bad because they are receiving thousands of gifts,
These big hosts are very thrifty in others' lives,
It's like this; they take and take and for every one hundred gifts they will only gift five out of that,
I wish I was joking but I'm not.

Woop Woop, the PK or TikTok Battles,
There will always be stingy buggers,
They have about one-hundred-thousand-followers,
Yet they won't gift, sorry got no gifts to give,
I'm like yeah, they will accept gifts but not give gifts,
Selfish and rude if ever they knew the meaning of those words.

So, when they finally gift someone,
I'm like oh my god you just gifted them,

Are you alright? Are you ill?
You just did something that was brill,
That ain't like you.

Happy Birthday

To all of you near and far,
Remember there is a story in every scar,
If you are looking for friendship,
You don't have to look much further,
You are my brother, the brother I never had,
Enjoy your day today,
Each birthday is only celebrated once a year,
Don't you shed a tear unless it's for joy,

I have been lucky enough to watch you grow,
As a person in this app,
The app is called clapper,
Not many people know about it,
Forget them,
You should be treated right,
For all the kindness you spread across the app,
So, let's all take a couple of seconds to clap for him,
His birthday is an important one,
One he didn't think he would make,
He not only made it he aced it,

There is still the rest of the day ahead,
After you have a nice long sleep in your bed,
Clear your mind and celebrate the generosity,
There's still nearly a whole day to live through,
It has been made extra special for you,
Each gift is appreciated big or small,
Everyone wishing him a happy birthday,
Wants him to have a birthday he'll never forget,
Don't forget about him just yet,

He still has lots to look forward too,
A birthday breakfast,
A wonderful birthday lunch,
Ending with a beautiful dinner,
Without forgetting his birthday cake,

You don't need to wish for diamonds,
You got them by the bucket load,
This is reality although it may feel like make believe,
Is the best birthday you have to ever receive?
It's not even half through,

I have a feeling you are going to have even more reason
To believe it is,
All you need now is some woman to kiss or to be kissed.

I can't

I can't go through heartbreak again,
No matter how much I practice zen,
It never seems to work,
I've got a bad cough,
Is this the beginning of the end?
It's kept me from sleeping,
I missed my dinner last night,
I am trying with all my might,

Will this be my last night?
My last day on earth?
If success meant that I fall by the wayside,
Than I don't want it,
Am I dying or am I just ill,
I am doing more than seven sources of income,
Yet only have one source,
I feel like walking through a forever revolving through door,
I don't want any more,

Am I sure?
Yeah, I am and I don't like it,
I feel like I won't make it to the end of November,
Let alone December,
I don't want to go back,
I want to go forward to the future,
See what happens is it worth living through,
I don't know about whether you feel can you survive,
I don't know whether I will survive let alone thrive,

It's like that song ironic,
They win the lottery,
Then they are turning into a mockery,
By dying and not leaving a will,
All they wanted was a thrill,
Pay for the food by going to the till,

Is it COVID.19 or is it not,
I always said to myself if it is I won't survive it it's only a bit of snot,
I might join the thirty-two club,
I aint speaking poker,
I wish I had the strength but I'm numb,

I am far from dumb,
By this COVID.19 doesn't discriminate,
No matter how much you hate,
If it was a person it wouldn't be your mate.

32 Club

If I go to sleep right now,
I'm afraid I would be gone,
No matter the amount of love,
I don't want to give it to anyone else,
It's a vicious beast,
They definitely aint fantastic,

To say that I will survive is an overstatement,
I can't battle this off,
It's like an alternate universe,
Where Goliath won against David,
Forget about Mavis,
This is one chase I won't win,
I aint got no twin,

Whenever someone says a number and then club,
Right after it, it means they name the age they die,
Forget the turkey I may die before December,
Let alone blame it on September or wake me up when it ends,
I aint sure whether I'll make it to the end of the week,
As I feel very ill no matter what,
Will anyone free from these chains dragging me down,
If I hid would anyone find me before it was too late,

It means nothing if I can't do anything to stop it,
So, goodnight poppet,
Know I always loved you,
Although I didn't always show it,
I always meant it when I said it,

Light a candle for me,
When it burns out that's when it will be,
Greta was right,
What's the point of living and learning,
If the sun will be burning the earth,
In one day like the speed of light,
It might happen,
The irony is everyone thinks COVID.19 will be the end of us,
Except it isn't it's the sun burning,
No amount of preparation is enough,
So, keep on being tough,
Like a diamond in the rough.

I can't get rid of this cough.
I go out once and already they are,
Arranging Christmas arrangements,
Like the periodic table of elements.

You

I am hanging on by a thread,
My feet are cold,
I heard you could catch gout if your blood,
Runs like veins in blue cheese,
Like mould,
So, I have put my fan on,
To heat up the atmosphere,
I am making everything crystal clear,
My dear,

I fear I have put the wrong type of fat on,
I look well I no longer look frail,
That is a tale for another time,
I thought grime meant dirt,
It doesn't though,
It means it's a type of music,
If music be the future,
Carry on its mutual,
It's a cheap thrill,
Until you get to the till,
It wasn't cheap after all,

If I could get told how many days,
Or weeks, months or years I had left,
Then I could live my life to the fullest,
While I countdown to my death,
Until my last breath,

I just want to know it,
Everyone says I won't take it for granted,
However, those are just words,
Just when you go a toilet, they are just turds,
I have heard you can't polish a turd,
Why would you want to anyway?
I've got three days to go till the weekend,
Will I make it or will it all end?

In September, when they were talking about the clapper meet,
I thought that's months away,
However, back then had you told me,
I would have a new community carer,
I would be like yeah ha-ha very funny,

However, it's true though now it's only one day away,
How quickly did that come around,
It's like I was wearing a crown,
Or a book waiting to release,
Don't try to please everyone,
You will fall short just like the hundred-to-one,
Horse in the grand national,
The reason they say find your niche,
Not everyone will like your videos,
There will be some who will though,
That's your audience,
That's your fam,
They will go crazy about your content,
Watching every video, you put up,

These people do exist,
You just need to experiment until you find that sweet spot,
When you hit the nail on the head,
That's where carry on with that content,
Where people will brag about your content by word of mouth,
Some people may think oh you just started on here,
I'm like NO I just have not found my niche.

Love It

This year's summer,
Is just a bummer,
Even a Hummer,
Tank Top,
On looking fleek,
My girlfriend gives me a kiss on the cheek.

Now is the time,
To get all of your summer clothes out,
To go about town out and about,
In your wheelchair,
Yeah what happened to jeans,
It's all about the track suit.

You see a woman at the café give you a wink,
She is hotter than you may think,
I attract women who haven't even had a drink.

What lasts longer on these days,
Love is not just some click and collect,
Money is love check and double check,
Love can be found in unexpected places,
You just need to keep playing those aces.

Like the wind which has an incredible force,
Love is running its course,
On the tennis courts,
No, it isn't false.

10K

It's not true,
That you become an expert,
At something after 10k hours,
Before the pandemic I spent way more than that,
Talking about dystonia on YouTube,
For who to?

I was doing a new video each day and editing it in iMovie,
I'm nowhere near an expert at it,
I had a niche which was dystonia,
Go and tell her,
Now I have no niche,
I am eating quiche,
Who knows what meat is in a shish (kebab),
No, I didn't say shush.

I currently have one-hundred-and-ninety subscribers,
Subscribers the most I have ever had,
For sure I miss dad,
I'm not the only one though,
Who is looking for that organic growth,
Although some people get one-thousand views on each video,
They ain't even using a video studio,
However, they don't have more subscribers than me,
That is the way it is meant to be.

I haven't broken four digits for a video yet,
But do I have a dream & believe in myself you bet,
A couple of viral videos & I should be all set,
No, I don't have a pet.

Thinking about owning a pet,
What and it molting and getting all wet,
A cat moults in the summer,
A gorilla can be a drummer,
Maybe that was what inspired the movie sing,
You don't want get stung,
By a wasp or a bee,
It doesn't matter if you're a he or a she,
Or non-binary.

Summer Serenade

It's way past the curfew,
For her she should be asleep,
She isn't a sheep,
Her parents didn't hear a peep,
Her boyfriend sent her a text,
Not a rock at her window,
Come on its twenty-twenty-one,
There had to be a new way of getting her attention.

Although this was not his initial intention,
The text said I'm outside your house,
How come you're still wearing your blouse,
I have been on a zoom call,
So, I wanted to look present-able.

Open your window so I can climb up,
Make sure I can have something in my cup,
Ok quieten up they may hear you,
Good thing I left my guitar here,
All I need for a good time is you, beer and both are already near.

Insatiable

You have expensive taste,
No time to waste,
We're on the case,
It's all for the adrenaline,
For the thrill of the chase,
When you get to have a taste,
It's not enough,
You want the whole cake,
I don't care what make,
I have to have it all.

I'm average height and not tall,
Why do some of the time I feel cool,
When others don't know I am not a tool,
If I was I would be a skeleton key,
As I have so many talents that belong to me.

I'm a jack of all trades,
However, I'm not getting paid for any,
Even though I have several streams of potential income,
So, I only get money when I win some,
I defeated the devil that is temptation,
I can't have a vacation,
The covid.19 vaccine put a stop to that,
I think while I adjust my hat.

The cashier gave me my winnings,
No, I ain't going swimming,
Why bother when I can't go abroad,
I will just sit here and watch mature cheddar turn into gorgonzola,
While having my Coca-Cola,
Classic although I don't mind the zero,
These NHS key workers should know they are heroes.

I buy one piece of clothing,
I think mum is gonna moan either way,
So, I might as well get what I can in the sale,
I'm not getting loads of money like Gareth Bale.

I just think what is the point of having the money in the bank,

If I died from corona virus by catching the delta variant,
Mum would get my money as she is next of kin,
She couldn't wear my clothes so I hope she wouldn't put them in the bin.

Before I went out I was like I won't spend much,
However, there were sales left, right and centre to touch,
I thought I can't miss out on this,
I've never seen so many sales it's like winning with a fist,
While playing rock and paper and scissors,
The prices were so cheap it was better than black Friday,
I'm guessing this is what they call a Fri-yay!

If Christmas Was Everyday

Just think about it for once,
In detail,
If Christmas was really every day,
Only the mega rich could afford it,
When would it stop?
It would be like Groundhog Day,
Where you have to pay for presents each time,
You would have to spend it more than dime,
It would cost a pretty penny,
So, there would only have to be two or three presents,
Each day,
Of course, the presents couldn't be expensive,
Like Harry Potter look inside the pensive,

You would get sick of it,
Imagine hearing Christmas songs,
Every day forever,
Make sure you have some lucky heather,
If you want to find the treasure,
It would be my pleasure,

Hell would freeze over,
Before this became true,
So, kick off your trainers,
Lay down and enjoy yourself,
Watching the TV,
Be who you want to be,
Watch what you want,

It isn't you can't,
It's just not now,
Bow down in front of royalty,
Don't be naughty,
Otherwise you won't be on Santa's nice list,
The naughty people only get a lump of coal,
I don't mean a coal pencil for your eyes that really bring out your eyes,
It costs nothing to be nice,
It costs nothing to be kind,
You just need to be in the right frame of mind,

If you can't say anything nice, don't say anything at all,
Otherwise they will stand tall leaving you standing small.
It ain't cool and it ain't clever,
You need to have a tough skin,
To face the world once you get famous,
You can't say you blame us,
Wear your mask while out in your wheelchair,
Do disabled people need to pay a fare?
I don't know it isn't clear,
Figure it out now it isn't worth a cheer.

Christmas Gifts

Bring me some gifts I can't afford,
Stand in front of the mirror,
You know I'm dapper,
Gift me on clapper,
I am happier,
Despite the gloomy situation,
That we are in,
You gotta love life,
It could always be worse,
Just remember that,
While you are holding on to your woolly hat,
So, it doesn't fly away in this strong gust of wind,

I'd like an apple watch, a new iPad mini,
A year of an apple TV+ subscription,
That is a prescription that would make me happy,
No, it ain't a drug some drugs are a placebo,
Ho, Ho, Ho,
Did you know?
Sometimes all it takes is a blind leap of faith,
To get better from feeling rock bottom,
No, I'm not a friend of Kelly Hoppen,

I'll have a meet and greet with Anastacia,
Once this pandemic goes and we can meet each other again,
Will it be all better by this time next year?
I think the earth needs a plaster and bandage fix its wounds,
That come from the coronavirus pandemic.

Christmas Magic

What makes Christmas a magical time of year?
Can you guess?
Well it's the Christmas music of course,
Like deck the halls,
Or baby it's cold outside,
Who can forget White Christmas?
No one.

I can't believe it took twenty-five years for Mariah Carey to get
To Christmas number one,
So, don't give up on your dreams,
Just yet,
Every year her song would get in the Christmas top 40,
Never number one though,
Until last year,

What is the moral of this,
Good things come to those wait,
You are just one failure away from success,
However, people are quitters and are impatient,
They want to get rich right here right now,
The world doesn't work that way,

People who have over a million subscribers on YouTube,
Took them nine or ten years to get that,
It didn't happen as easy as pulling a rabbit out of a hat,
It happened by you interacting which each other regularly,
The more you speak to them,
They will think this bloke seems quite nice,
I'm going to be one of his subscribers,

The key to all success on social media is engagement,
If you just watch their videos but don't comment, like their video or select all notifications,
They aint going to remember you,
Unless you are flamboyant,
The key is to be different,
IF you are you and you are already unique,
That's the technique to originality,
It's what keeps them coming back,
Time and time again.

It's Going to Make History

Harry Kane will score sometime in the match,
However, don't get too attached,
As Italy has been here before,
That doesn't matter though,
If the queen is backing England,
And it ain't even in Poland.

If England win it we cry tears of joy,
If we are on the edge of our seats we will still enjoy,
I'm just sitting here eating chips ahoy,
Time to score a goal again,
It's with this that I say amen.

Harry Maguire is looking to bounce,
Sixty-thousand people in the crowd,
I believe there are quite a lot of Britons,
Thinking about the past is forbidden.
The future isn't written,
So, don't act smitten.

Move, pass left to right,
The championship final is being played tonight,
So, don't put it out of your sight,
Can Rahim Sterling bring it home he just might?

The Italians have the end in sight,
Even if some of them are tall,
They won't win at all,
If they score one goal it will still be too small.

Harry Kane is a G.O.A.T,
Just passed Gary Lineker,
In this EURO 2020,

He never fails,
He never misses,
From what I have seen,
If you haven't where have you been?
To be a teen in this life,
Is it like an edge of a knife?
Far from strife.

Fake It to Make It

Oh yeah England will win,
I say while I put betting slips in the bin,
Mum wants me to die as she is next of kin,
I ain't going anywhere so you won't get a thing,
Did you hurt your shin?

I bet Italy would win in June,
Even though I don't eat a Prune,
It's the final I bet on both,
England or Italy will win,
So, no matter the outcome get money,
It was less if England won,
My Italy bet was already done.

I won my money back plus twenty-six-pound profit,
Nothing could stop it,
Watch it my prediction was three-to-one,
The bet was won,
If England did,
I would have got nine-pound less,
So, guess how much I bet?

I used to love Jet,
From gladiators in the nineties,
What a throwback,
A lot of you weren't even born,
I say as I think of postman-pat,
Who always delivers,
Never gives me the shivers.

Best Wishes Dad (Rest in Peace)

I always wanted to go fishing with dad,
He always said no even when he was well,
Could you tell?
Thanks for the television,
I would chat to him like my life depended on it,
In a way it did except the opposite,
Happened and he died in his sleep.

He didn't even have a jeep,
He spent his whole life wanting a sports car,
He finally got one and then went in the dark,
No spark, no last words, nothing, he died fast,
Mum slept in the same bed,
He was dead she scratched her head,
At ten o'clock in the morning he was ice cold and dead,
Nothing else could really be said then,

However, I prepared a eulogy to read out at his funeral,
I would feel bad and regret it if I let the time past me by,
So, I spoke from the head and the heart,
As your emotions come from both,
I hope he could now rest in peace the most.

All of these things happening,
Is it coming from a re-awakening?
I inhaled the hate and exhaled the love,
So, all of the hate turned into affection,
Have I got your attention?
When are we having that melon,
I haven't a clue, I don't know anyone called Helen.

Hey Sis (You'll Be Fine)

If you've got a talent use it,
Or as they say if you don't use it lose it,
The things I do get taken for granted,
You can't spell granted without ranted,
Everyone has their chance to moan,
Just to set the tone,
I'll speak to you on the phone,
I won't drone,
I will try to make you laugh,
Even though you might be wearing a mask.

What do I have to ask?
If all else fails talk about the weather,
Or whether you got some lucky heather,
Do you think I'm clever?
What do you have for lunch,
Let them guess you went to the Wetherspoons?
Are you making all of the guys swoon?
The radio is on and they are playing your current favourite tune!

Stop thinking everyone is happy like they are in Walt Disney World,
When this couldn't be farther than the truth they are just posers,
Some of them are boring and make up what they did they are just losers,
They ain't royalty they can't have done much in an evening or a weekend,
If you question them you may find out that it was all pretend,
How will you find out? When you hit a nerve and they are quick to defend.

Let's this be the end of you thinking they are god's gift,
You couldn't be further from the truth they are a thrift,
They want you to think they are having a great time,
The truth is they probably haven't even spent a dime.
Big Ben chimes sixteen times an hour make sure you don't waste even one of
them.

Star or Nobody

Would you rather be a star or nobody?
You could be a singer who has perfect pitch,
No, I'm not called mitch,
Now don't get a stitch,
Would you want to be a somebody or nobody?
If I got the perks that a somebody gets,
Otherwise I wouldn't want to be somebody that people easily forget,

I would want to have a star named after me,
That would be so cool just like if I was a golfer taking his first swing from the tee,
I am good at golf except on the PlayStation I was like 'dad look that's me',
Hehe 'I know son' love from dad,
What I good time we both had,
Dad said 'son stay strong',
'Go get yourself a girlfriend',
I forget about what was wrong.

I went to the supermarket,
I got more than I bargained for,
I would love a girlfriend while going on a tour,
Around the supermarket,
For sure,
I want more,
This woman was walking in front of me,
I thought she is wearing thongs,

I don't mean thongs,
I mean flip flops,
I ain't in Australia,
Who knows what if it is Santa mailing 'ya,
Where is my face mask sample in the mail or courier?
I have one left out of two,
I lost my blue face mask I had it for nearly two years,
Oh well, I still have the talent of design,
It's takes time for it arrive; once it's arrived its mine,
I treated it like fine wine,
However, I didn't drink it,
As I can't drink alcohol!

One Hundred

Usain bolt whole career was about getting under ten or twenty seconds,
Did he train for four years to get that record or records?
No, I don't mean LPs,
I said mum can we have LP player,
Oh, come on mum don't be a hater,
Maybe she will change her mind later.

Dad may have passed away,
But the days keep rolling on,
You can't hit pause on life,
Even if you are having strife.

Life is no rolling phone contract,
That you can cancel when it no longer meets your needs,
The phone company will keep taking money like how venus flytrap feeds,
I never liked babybel,
However, I like dairylea I know they are both barely cheese,
Aren't they like ninety-seven percent milk,
Best served chilled and I ain't talking beer,
England just got another goal here,
How many caps for England does Harry Kane have.

Why are they saying it's eighteen-months to the world cup?
I'd love me to have a Labrador pup,
I'm pretty sure the world cup is in June and July,
Which is only twelve months away,
What do they say?
Not it ain't in may!

I just had a quick search,
It's way too early for England merch,
I will wear my England shirt,
Oh my god,
The football world cup is in November twenty-two,
Will I remember?

Maybe in November it's summer in Qatar,
Have you seen my massive scar?
On my arm,
What's this?
England might not get to play in the World Cup,

As the England fans didn't take it kindly losing Euro 2020,
The violence may jeopardise their presence in the World Cup,
Qatar won't put up with it,
People are blindly thinking we qualify for the World Cup,
Our football skills should come first,
Instead of the fists,
Instead of the violence.

Adrenaline or Dopamine

When you do something that turns out good,
Is it adrenaline or dopamine that gives the energy,
Maybe it's a synergy,
A mix of both of them,
Or could it be from the split hem,
Of your pencil skirt,
Are you hurt?
No just my ego is bruised,
There ain't no excuse.

I can't stay here now,
It won't be long till the shirt completely rips in two,
Do I believe Jensen Ackles is really on clapper?
That would be so cool if he was,
It could be a catfish I mean anyone can put a profile pic and bio,
Who knows they could be from Ohio.

Adrenaline is when something comes overbearing to you,
Which you either fight or flight or stay or run away,
So that you can live another day,
Did you know a coffee can either keep you awake?
Or send you to sleep,
Coffee is a stimulant,
Which can stimulate your senses,
For many hours afterwards but nothing can replace sleep,
Who has ever had success with counting sheep.

There will always be someone who is against you,
Why does it have to be the person who determines your growth,
The most important one on the most visited websites on the web,
No, they are not called deb,
Yes, the chairman of the Olympics is called seb.

Dopamine is realised when you are happy,
So this is why people often say spend your life doing what makes you happy,
Otherwise your life could go from happy to crappy,
Don't do the job that someone wants you to do,

Take the bull by the horns and do the job you want to,
Don't pretend you got the flu,

One day you will get a bad strain of it,
People won't believe you,
They will be like you had it the other week,
What are the chances of getting it again,
Did you catch it from a friend?
When will this end,
Don't lie where you can't easily tend,
To remember what happened.

ACKNOWLEDGEMENTS

Thank you so much to my family and my wacky life for providing experiences to express in poem form. They say things happen for a reason and if it never happened I wouldn't have been able to write these poems. Not all of the poems were written in the pandemic. A lot were written in the lockdown like the Christmas poems, more or less all of the Christmas poems were written in the pandemic.

I am all for turning a negative into a positive. I think everyone will agree that we didn't want the pandemic; but just like Elton John who wrote a whole album in the pandemic and lockdown.

Any trolls that I experienced just made me have keener to write more poems and get on and become more successful. I ain't going to be taken down by a single troll. They want a reaction, they want you to mute or block them because the majority of them have multiple accounts so if you block one of their accounts, they will just use one of their other accounts.

Respond to them; then f* *k* *g ignore them. I haven't spent weeks of my time growing my account for it to be taken down due to trolls.

So, thanks for spurring me on, you didn't expect this a second book in the same year.

I have made this book clean covering up any swear words while still keeping the meaning of them I hope.

Let's see how well this book does, even if it only sells one copy that's one more than none. It has been fun writing this book, so hopefully this becomes a hard back so you can hold it in your hands, which you couldn't do with my first novel.

However, I have to say thank you to Amazon if it manages to publish this book as a hardback as it says that hardback editions are in BETA.

If I can't get it turned as a hardback, I will get it published as a paperback. Why this poem book is especially poignant to me is because I had written a fifty-page poem book about ten years ago but it got lost and I had no back up.

Not all of these poems are based on real experiences; however most of them are. I'll leave that up for you to figure out which ones are real and which ones are fictional.

Once these poems are published to the world they become yours and how you can relate to them or not. Okay, I have written every poem but people interpret them in all different ways, no one will experience in the same way that's what good about how diverse the poems are.

I heard that 3am to 4am in the early hours is the witching hour so maybe a higher power was helping me. Not an actual human though. Decide by yourself whether you think this is true.

They say I was the first person in my family to complete their degree at university, maybe I'm the first person to become an author and a poet too in my family.

I truly hope it is a success. It has taken countless hours to complete this book that why I don't think it is true about the ten thousand hours myth. I mean you are even a poet and have the talent or not. Like with singers, you can either sing or not.

Some of my poems are very long but that is because I got carried away and run with it, the muse that inspires mean to write poems.

I mean 100% my muse is other musicians and their music as it gets me in the creative mood. I just got a message from Dua Lipa on Spotify for listening to her and Don't Start Now making it on my Wrapped.

ABOUT THIS POETRY BOOK

There's a selection of different poems to read, each one is different this is why I couldn't do a content as each poem is about a different subject, and there's one poem per page or per two pages. I have tried to cut down on the length of some of the poems but I couldn't get my point across in just one page. If you love reading and you love poems, you are going to love this book.

If you don't like the sound of one poem, just turn the page to the next one there's plenty to read. There is loads to read that is why it is the perfect present for Christmas there are loads of different subjects; over 40 pages of Christmas poems as long as a Birthday one and an Easter one in this book.